100 FACTS

Man Utd

First published in Great Britain in 2015
by Wymer Publishing
www.wymerpublishing.co.uk
Wymer Publishing is a trading name of Wymer (UK) Ltd

ISBN 978-1-908724-15-1

Edited by John Kemp.

Typeset by Wymer.
Printed and bound by Lightning Source.

A catalogue record for this book is available from the British Library.

Cover design by Wymer.
Sketches by Becky Welton. © 2014.

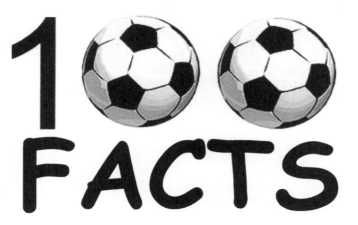

FACTS

Man Utd

Iain McCartney

WYMER
PUBLISHING
Bedford, England

BEFORE THE RED DEVILS THERE WAS A GOAT AND A GOOSE

Manchester United's modern day mascot is a red devil who goes by the name of 'Fred the Red'. Similar figures at other clubs are not something simply conjured up by the modern day game, as mascots have been around for many years. Even Newton Heath had one.

But the Heathens mascot was not some furry, costumed dressed supporter, but was advertised as 'the singing canary'. Thankfully there was no trade's description act back in those distant days, as it was in fact a goose and nothing more than a ploy to make the odd penny during hard times at the fledgling club. Sadly 'Michael' was to become someone's Christmas dinner.

Next up was captain Harry Stafford's St Bernard's Dog, 'Major' who was indeed a 'lucky mascot', wandering into a pub owned by J H Davies, whose daughter took a liking to the dog. An

agreement was reached with Stafford allowing his dog to stay in exchange for Davies putting money into the beleaguered Newton Heath, with the club changing its name to Manchester United soon afterwards.

Billy the goat, whose stuffed head can be seen in the United Museum, was a much bigger attraction than the previously mentioned 'canary', as he would parade around the ground before games. Then after the final whistle, follow the players to a nearby public house, where he had the tendency to drink too much before falling over. After the 1909 cup final, he actually died of alcoholic poisoning.

A large teddy bear can also be seen in some team pictures during the 1920s! Human mascots were soon to be regular features, with 'Hoppy' Thorne, who had lost a leg during the First World War, becoming United's first, hopping along the touch line. Occasionally his false leg would remain in place and he would run around the pitch perimeter.

He was succeeded by Jack Irons, a red and white clad figure who would parade around the pitch and often toss the coin before kick-off.

Fred the Red is nothing but a poor imitation of his predecessors.

A
TESTING
TIME

In the early days of the Football League, promotion and relegation was decided by 'Test Matches', fore-runners of the modern day 'play-offs'. Prior to that there was no automatic promotion or relegation whatsoever.

Newton Heath were to find themselves involved in those 'Test Matches' at the end of the 1892-93 season when they finished 16th in the top flight; 1893-94 when they again finished 16th; the 1894-95 season, when they finished third in the Second Division and in 1896-97 when they were runners-up in the Second Division.

In 1892-93, they faced Small Heath at Stoke, drawing 1-1, while in the replay at Bramall Lane, Sheffield, they enjoyed a convincing 5-2 victory to consolidate their place in the First Division. The following season, they were not so fortunate, as they were beaten 2-0 by Liverpool at Ewood Park, Blackburn, and were subsequently relegated.

Attempting to spring back immediately, finishing third in Division Two, their hopes of promotion were shattered by Stoke City at Port Vale, losing 3-0.

In 1896-97, things had changed slightly, with four games now required to be played. In the first of the quartet against Burnley, they lost 2-0 away, but won 2-0 at home. Three days later, they were up against Sunderland and were held to a 1-1 draw at home, but were to lose the return in the north-east 2-0, thus ending any hopes of a return to the top flight.

Much to the Heathens relief, the 'Test Matches' were soon to be abandoned, with straight forward promotion and relegation deciding the fate of all clubs. But it was not until 1905-06 that managed to step out of the Second Division as runners-up.

SMOKE GETS IN YOUR EYES

FACT **3**

Newton Heath played their initial fixtures at North Road, Monsall, a far from ideal venue where the ground could be a mud heap, or in the middle of winter, frozen solid. The changing rooms were half a mile away at the Three Crowns public house, meaning that both teams had to walk to and from the ground in the playing kit no matter what the weather might be.

In 1893, the Heathens moved to Bank Street, Clayton, that had a grandstand, which could accommodate 1000 spectators: In reality, the only improvement for the hardened support. Actual playing conditions were still far from ideal.

The ground lay adjacent to the local chemical works, where smoke billowed from the huge chimneys, filling the ground with obnoxious smells. It is also documented that if the Heathens were losing on a Saturday afternoon, the worker in charge of the boilers would be informed and the smoke and smells would become even greater in an attempt to upset the visiting players.

Such were the poor conditions that following a 14-0 victory over Walsall Town Swifts, the visitors complained about the condition of the ground and the atrocious weather. The game was ordered to be replayed and on this occasion Newton Heath only scored nine without reply.

THE FAN THAT
FED THE PLAYERS

Present day support for Manchester United is legendary, but even in the early days of the fledgling Newton Heath club, there were a number of staunch supporters, especially from the various departments of the Lancashire and Yorkshire Railway, eager to encourage their workmates. But two of the most faithful followers from that distant past were 'Father' Bird and Mr. Sedgwick.

Bird, despite his name, was not a priest, but the local chimney sweep and he would regularly invite the players back to his house for a post-match meal of potato pie, or Lancashire hot-pot, followed by some refreshments and a sing-song.

Mr Sedgwick on the other hand, was the station master at Victoria Station and with the club's railway connections, he always made sure that for travel to away fixtures, reserved accommodation was secured for the players and club officials, allowing them to travel in both comfort and style.

THE
DISAPPEARING PLAYERS

Floodlights were not installed at Old Trafford until March 1957, but they did make a much earlier appearance at Clayton, although only briefly.

For his services to the club, captain Harry Stafford, along with team mate Walter Cartwright was awarded a benefit match and the pair decided on the novel and perhaps the added attraction, of playing the match against neighbours Manchester City under 'Wells Lights' – a series of lamps strung up on poles around the pitch, along with a gilded ball.

A brave and innovative decision, but on the night in question there was a rather strong wind and no sooner were the lights illuminating the playing arena than one would be blown out. This would be re-lit only for another to be extinguished and so it continued until the ground was completely enveloped in darkness, forcing the referee to abandon the match.

Upon reaching the dressing rooms, it was discovered that many of the players were already there, washed and changed, having simply walked off in the semi-darkness, their absence going un-noticed.

THE ST BERNARD DOG THAT HELPED CREATE MANCHESTER UNITED

FACT **6**

Players earning thousands of pounds per week, with match day gate receipts of over £1m are commonplace today, but in those distant days of Newton Heath, the financial side of things was so much different.

Such were the difficulties surrounding the club, that door to door collections in the Newton Heath area were made in order to secure the train fares for the players to make the next away fixture, while en-route to those away games, the pre-match meal would often consist of a bottle of beer and a piece of cheese.

With money really tight, players were often paid according to the gate receipts, with players often having to revert to pawning their only suit until a Saturday evening. It was also not unknown for a player to feign injury to avoid playing at all, if it was thought that the afternoon's takings were going to mean little or no pay whatsoever.

One fundraising idea when faced with bankruptcy was a Bazaar in St James Hall and it was in connection with this that the legend of the St Bernard's dog arose.

Various versions of events surrounding 'Major' have evolved, from the dog wandering off on its own, to being locked in an upstairs room before escaping. But what is certain, is that the daughter of brewery owner Mr J. H. Davies took a liking to Harry Stafford's pet and a deal was struck between the two men. Davies obtained the dog for his daughter and Stafford secured funds for his team in exchange, with Davies becoming chairman of a newly formed club – Manchester United.

NEWTON HEATH
FACT 7 BECOMES MANCHESTER UNITED

It was on 24 April 1902, during a meeting in the New Islington Public Hall, in the Ancoats area of the city, that it was decided to change the name of Newton Heath Football Club to that of Manchester United.

One of the reasons behind the change of name was that numerous visiting supporters and teams, unfamiliar with the city, had made their way to Newton Heath only to find that they were a few miles away from the club home in Clayton.

One team had turned up at the club's previous ground on North Road only to find nothing there and by the time they managed to find alternative transport over to Bank Street Clayton, it was five minutes prior to kick-off.

The change of name was put forward by M. J. Brown who was chairing the meeting, while another suggested name was Manchester Celtic. A vote saw 'United' being the favoured choice, although one or two were opposed to any change at all.

The last league fixture under the name of Newton Heath was a 2-0 home win over Chesterfield on April 23 1902, while Manchester United began life with a 1-0 victory at Gainborough Trinity. Charlie Richards scoring that first 'United' goal.

THEY THOUGHT THEY WEREN'T GOALIES...
THEY ARE NOW

Before multiple substitutes were allowed it caused immense problems if the goalkeeper went off injured. United have been caught out on a handful of occasions, relying on an outfield player to pull on the number one shirt in that hour of need.

Rio Ferdinand took over in goal during an FA Cup quarter-final at Portsmouth in March 2008, after Edwin van der Sar went off injured and his replacement Tomasz Kuszczak was sent off, but the central defender could do little to keep United in the competition.

In February 2007, John O'Shea deputised for van der Sar at White Hart Lane, when United had used all three substitutes. He made one notable stop from Robbie Keane.

Others who have deputised in goal are, Alex Dawson, replacing Harry Gregg in the 2-0 home win against Spurs in 1961; David Herd against Liverpool in November 1963 and Blackburn two years later. David Sadler replaced Alex Stepney at Highbury in August 1970 and Brian Greenhoff likewise at Birmingham in 1972. Duncan Edwards also briefly kept goal in the 1956 FA Charity Shield against Man City, replacing Ray Wood, before David Gaskell came on for his debut.

Perhaps the most high profile was Jackie Blanchflower in the 1957 FA Cup Final against Aston Villa, when Ray Wood was injured. Casting up the trivia question "Who was the only outfield player ever to wear a cap in a Wembley Cup Final?" Blanchflower did so to shield his eyes from the bright sunlight. Blanchflower was not unfamiliar with goalkeeping, having played a friendly against Helsingborg on 8 May 1956.

However, Johnny Carey played in goal for the whole 90 minutes of a First Division fixture at Sunderland in February 1953, replacing Ray Wood who took ill on the day.

GOALKEEPER
TURNED POACHER

Not only have United goalkeepers earned the plaudits for keeping the ball out of the net, they have also been known to score the odd goal or two.

During season 1973-74, Alex Stepney was at one point joint leading scorer with 2 goals. Having scored from the penalty spot in a pre-season friendly against Penarol, he was nominated as the team's penalty taker once the league season got underway and scored from the spot against Leicester City and Birmingham City.

He failed to make it a hat trick of penalty strikes, missing from the spot against Wolverhampton Wanderers. Harry Gregg also scored from the spot during a friendly, beating his opposite number in the Ukrainian National side in Philadelphia in June 1960.

Peter Schmeichel, however, didn't need a penalty award to find the net, as he headed home a corner against Rotor Vologograd in the 1995-96 UEFA Cup at Old Trafford.

Harry Moger also managed to get his name on the score sheet, in the post 1907-08 season tour, scoring in the 7-0 victory over Hungarian side Ferencvaros on May 24th.

THE FIRST SUBSTITUTES

Substitutes were first used in the Football League at the start of the 1965-66 season, when they were only allowed to be used in the event of an injury to an out-field player.

United's first named substitute was Willie Anderson for the FA Charity Shield match against Liverpool on 14 August 1965. He was called into action in the 16th minute, replacing Denis Law. The home match against Sheffield Wednesday on 21 August, the opening day of that particular season, saw Noel Cantwell named as United's first League substitute. The Irishman was not, however, called into action. It was not until 16 October at White Hart Lane that United's first League substitute was sent onto the pitch, with John Fitzpatrick replacing the injured Denis Law against Tottenham Hotspur.

Substitutions in friendly fixtures were a different matter altogether and often simply down to the clubs involved as to how many they could use. In one particular friendly, against Eintracht Frankfurt in Los Angeles on 17 May 1970, United, or perhaps Francis Burns, created something of a record for the number of substitutions in one game.

Starting the game against the Germans at left half, he was replaced during the game by Steve James, only to reappear soon afterwards as a replacement for right back Paul Edwards. Burns was then once again removed from the action to allow Willie Watson to come on. Thankfully, he had not gone and got into the shower, as he was soon back into the thick of things, taking the place of right half Pat Crerand. This time, he managed to remain on the pitch until full time.

UNITED GREAT
CYCLED TO MATCHES

Duncan Edwards is still talked about today as the greatest player ever to pull on the red shirt of Manchester United. He was a mere boy of 16 years and 185 days, when he made his first team debut against Cardiff City at Old Trafford on 4 April 1953.

The boy from Dudley in the West Midlands went on to make 175 appearances, scoring 21 goals before his untimely death in the Rechts der Isar hospital in Munich fifteen days after the fateful crash that destroyed a Manchester United team who were on the verge of greatness. He had also made fifteen appearances for England following his debut as an 18 year old.

However, did you know that the United and England star also had a criminal record?

One evening, whilst returning to his digs after visiting his girlfriend Molly Leach, he was stopped by a policeman for riding his bicycle without any lights. He was subsequently taken to court and fined ten shillings (50p) for law breaking.

Duncan and his bicycle were also a common sight on match days, as he would cycle to the ground, tie the bike with a piece of string to a drain pipe outside the main entrance before going to the dressing room to prepare for the game that afternoon.

FACT 12
BARGAIN BUY
DELIVERS THE GOODS

After becoming manager in February 1946 Matt Busby's first signing was Jimmy Delaney. Many considered the Scot, who cost £4,000 when signed from Glasgow Celtic was past his best. Not simply because he was 32 years old, but also due to the fact that he had suffered a serious arm injury while playing for the Parkhead side. As a consequence they had struggled to find insurance cover for the player.

United obtained the necessary cover and Delaney went on to play over 180 games for the club, winning an FA Cup winners medal in 1948.

Delaney had won a Scottish Cup winners medal with Celtic in 1937 and in 1954 he added an Irish Cup winner's medal while playing with Derry City. He also narrowly missed out in making it a quadruple. Having crossed the Irish border into the Republic, he had to be content with a runners up medal as player-manager with Cork Athletic in 1955-56.

It is interesting to note that United's initial outlay for Jimmy Delaney was all but £500 recouped, when he was sold to Aberdeen for £3,500 in November 1950.

FACT 13 CROSSING THE GREAT DIVIDE

Crossing the divide between Manchester United and Manchester City is something that only a few players have done. For some the move has been accepted, but for others they have been despised for life, even if the move has not been a direct switch between the two clubs.

Some of the names are familiar, like that of Denis Law and Billy Meredith, but amongst the others are Brain Kidd (currently a City coach), Sandy Turnbull, Jimmy Bannister, Herbert Burgess, George Livingstone, Peter Barnes, Harry Rowley, Andy Cole, Peter Schmeichel, John Gidman, Terry Cooke, Bert Read, William Douglas, Bill Riding, Len Langford, Dan Hurst, Fred Williams, Bob Milarvie, Adam Carson, Joe Cassidy, Frank Buckley, Wilf Woodcock, Frank Barret, Herbert Bloomfield, Hugh Morgan, Peter Bodack, Sammy McIlroy, Peter Beardsley, Frank Knowles, John Christie, George Albinson, Billy Dale, Carlos Tevez, Wyn Davies, Mark Robins, Andrei Kanchelskis.

The highest transfer fee between the two clubs was the £600,000 City paid United for Terry Cooke in April 1999, while United paid City £500,000 in January 1996 for goalkeeper Tony Coton, but he was never to feature at first team level before being transferred to Sunderland. He later returned to Old Trafford as goalkeeping coach.

Shaun Goater and Tony Whelan played for both clubs, but did not feature in the United first team in a competitive fixture. Goater was to become something of a legend in the light blue shirt.

FACT 14

SPECTATOR PLAYS AGAINST CITY

Manchester United's youngest post-war player was goalkeeper David Gaskell, who was only 16 years and 19 days when he came on as substitute for Ray Wood in the FA Charity Shield match against Manchester City at Maine Road.

Gaskell had travelled to the game on public transport, simply as a spectator, but following Wood's injury, one of the United coaching staff remembered seeing the youngster going into the ground and a call was put out for him to come to the United dressing room.

Borrowing a pair of boots, he took his place between the posts, performing admirably, keeping a clean sheet as United won 1-0, performing so well in fact, that everyone assumed that Ray Wood had simply returned to the fray.

After the game he returned to his digs by bus, with supporters who had been at the game, all of whom were completely unaware that their fellow passenger had actually played in the match.

Gaskell was to win a second medal with United some seven years later, playing in the 3-1 FA Cup Final victory over Leicester City.

UNITED'S FIRST
BLACK PLAYER

Black players are now part and parcel of the modern game and it is now almost unusual for a team not to have any black players in its line-up.

Today we have the likes of Rio Ferdinand, Valencia, Anderson, Young, Nani, Smalling and Rafael in the squad, with others such as Dwight Yorke, Andy Cole, Wes Brown, Paul Parker, Viv Anderson, Paul McGrath and Remi Moses adding to the ranks over the years. Another was Paul Ince, the first black player to captain the club.

But the first black player to play first team football for Manchester United was Dennis Walker, who made his first team debut against Bolton Wanderers in Cork in February 1963.

He was to make only one solitary competitive appearance for the club, against Nottingham Forest on the final day of the 1962-63 season.

THE FRENCHMAN'S BAD BEHAVIOUR THAT COST UNITED THE LEAGUE

Eric Cantona was sent off while playing for Manchester United five times in fifteen months, between November 1993 and January 1995. Two of those dismissals came in successive matches, at Swindon Town on 19 March 1994 and at Arsenal on 22 March 1994 and as a result he was banned for five games.

One of his other sending's off came against Crystal Palace on 25 January 1995 for kicking out at Richard Shaw. Having been red carded by the referee, Cantona was leaving the pitch and walking towards the dressing rooms, when he was subjected to a torrent of abuse from a supporter in the crowd. Cantona reacted immediately, launching himself kung-fu style over the hoardings and towards the supporter, before aiming a number of punches in his direction.

Following this attack, he was arrested and charged with assault and following an appearance in court was given a two-week gaol sentence. This was eventually overturned on appeal to 120 hours community service.

United suspended the player for the remainder of the season and fined him £20,000; a suspension and fine which was increased by the Football Association to eight months and a further £10,000.

Due to the Frenchman's absence, United lost the league title to Blackburn Rovers.

LAW UNTO
HIMSELF

Denis Law was a British record signing when Matt Busby bought him from Italian side Torino £110,000 for his signature in the summer of 1962. A year after he had become the world's first £100,000 transfer when he joined Torino from Manchester City.

Busby had been well aware of Law's talents from his days as a Huddersfield Town player, as he was Scotland team boss, when at Cardiff in October 1956, the Aberdonian became the youngest post-war Scotland debutant at the age of 18. He was still pulling on the dark blue shirt in 1974.

At Old Trafford, he scored seven minutes into his debut against West Bromwich Albion and created numerous records in his eleven years at the club.

Between 1965 and 1969, he scored a then club record 14 goals in the European Cup and again in all European competitions between 1963 and 1969 with 28.

Up until 1996, 22 years after retiring, he held the record of the most prolific goal scorer in the FA Cup, with 41. He is the only man ever to score six goals in an FA Cup tie, yet finish on the losing side. The half dozen goals coming for Manchester City against Luton Town in January 1961 in a game that was abandoned due to the state of the pitch with City winning 6-2. Luton won the re-arranged match 3-1.

Law captained United to two League championships and was United's top scorer in five different seasons. His record of 18 career hat-tricks for United still stands. In season 1963-64, he scored seven hat tricks and has notched a hat trick in the European Cup, European Cup

Winners Cup and the Inter Cities Fairs Cup.

In 1963, he scored against the same goalkeeper, Gordon Banks, at Wembley on three different occasions, playing for three different teams. For United against Leicester City in the FA Cup final, for the Rest of the World against England, and for Scotland against England.

Along with George Best and Bobby Charlton, he has been named as *European Footballer of the Year*.

Unknown to many, Denis Law is the only United player to have two statues in his honour (three if you count one in Aberdeen), with the 'Trinity' at the front of the ground and another inside the Stretford End.

Not a bad career for someone who played his early football wearing glasses due to asquint in one eye!

SIMPLY
THE
BEST

FACT **18**

George Best played in four different countries in the space of 10 days whilst with Fulham. League fixtures at Craven Cottage and Ninian Park Cardiff. A friendly in Scotland against St Johnstone and a Northern Ireland international fixture in Belfast, but it is as a Manchester United player that he is best remembered, enjoying a successful, but sometimes controversial career at Old Trafford.

He is the only player to top the Manchester United scoring charts for five successive seasons – 1967-68 until 1971-72 and in the first of those campaigns he was named as the *Football Writers Footballer of the Year* and the *European Footballer of the Year*.

On 7 February 1970, against Northampton Town in an FA Cup fifth round tie, an 8-2 victory, he became only the second Manchester United player to score 6 goals in a game. His first goal for the club had come on 28 December 1963 in the 5-1 win over Burnley, with his first FA Cup goal against Barnsley on 15 February 1964.

In all, he scored 178 goals in 466 appearances.

FROM MINER TO
EUROPEAN CUP HERO

The career of United defender Bill Foulkes spanned that of the legendary 'Busby Babes' side of the pre-Munich period and the European Cup winning side of 1968.

Between 1956 and 1969, he played in 35 European Cup ties, a record that stood until broken by Peter Schmeichel in 1999. His equalising goal in the 3-3 second leg, semi-final tie of the 1968 competition in Madrid took United into the Final. In all, he was to play in 52 games in all European competitions, another record which stood for thirty years.

In the FA Cup, his 61 appearances were made in consecutive games, a record which will stand for all time.

The former miner from St Helens, escaped unhurt from the Munich disaster and played a major part in the team's recovery, captaining the side in the aftermath and during the following season. In that 1957-58 season, he played in every league, cup and European fixture.

Foulkes, like his team mates and every other player from that era, earned nothing like the wages of those players of today and he was one of the first footballers to put his medals and items up for auction.

At *Christies* in Glasgow in October 1992, his European Cup winner's medal sold for £11,000, with the blue number five jersey he wore that night raising £1,800. In all, twenty items went under the hammer, earning the player around £35,000.

Rather ironically, the medal was re-sold in November 2012 for £40,000.

UNITED'S
TARTAN ARMY

Tommy Docherty was manager of the Scottish national side prior to taking over from Frank O'Farrell as manager in December 1972. It was perhaps not simply a coincidence that he bought seven Scottish players – George Graham, Alex Forsyth, Jim Holton and Lou Macari within weeks of taking on the United job, as well as George Buchan, Stewart Houston and Jim McCalliog. He also introduced Arthur Albiston into the first team.

It was little wonder that tartan scarves became part of the Old Trafford match-day dress code at the time. Even more so when the team that faced West Ham United at Old Trafford on 20 January 1973 contained no fewer than eight players who had played for the Scottish national side – Alex Forsyth, Jim Holton, Martin Buchan, George Graham, Willie Morgan, Lou Macari, Denis Law and Ted MacDougall.

Five of those players were also to line up for Scotland against England the following month, but they took their club form north to Hampden with them, as the visitors ran out 5-0 winners.

GOAL SCORING MACHINE
IS NO JACK OF ALL TRADES

Jack Rowley was a noted goal scorer in Matt Busby's immediate post-war team, playing 422 games and scoring 208 goals. He made something of a headline hitting start to his United career after signing from Bournemouth for £3,000 in October 1937. He scored four against Swansea Town in what was only his second game. His 30 goals during the 1951-52 championship winning campaign was a record that stood until 1959-60 when Dennis Viollet scored 32.

But in the war time seasons, there were occasions when he seemed to score goals for fun.

In the latter stages of season 1940-41, he scored 14 goals in six of the final seven games. This fine vein of form continued into the following season when, in the opening weeks of season 1941-42, he scored an amazing 33 goals in the first 15 fixtures. No mean feat, when you consider that he failed to score in four of those games!

In the first game of that particular season he scored 7 against a hapless New Brighton in a 13-1 game, going on to score 4 on three occasions and 5 on another.

UNITED'S FIRST ENGLAND PLAYER

Charlie Roberts became the first Manchester United player to be capped by England in 1905, winning three caps against Ireland, Wales and Scotland.

Roberts joined United in April 1904 for a fee reported to be £600 from Grimsby Town. Six foot tall and strongly built, Roberts went on to become club captain.

He guided his team to its first League Championship in 1908 and first FA Cup success a year later, as well as a second title success in 1911. As well has his three full England caps, he also won eight Football League caps and played in four England trial matches.

A superb all-round defender, with a quick burst of speed, he was to become chairman of the Professional Footballers Association. He left United for Oldham Athletic in August 1913, having made 299 appearances, and scoring 23 goals

He later owned a tobacconist business where he sold *Ducrobel* cigars, named after the United half back line in which he played – Duckworth, Roberts and Bell.

A CAREER MEASURED
IN SECONDS

When a player starts out in the professional game, they usually look forward to a long and successful playing career at whatever level they play at. However, not all achieve this.

As far as United are concerned, the shortest career is that of goalkeeper Nick Culkin, who replaced Raimond van der Gouw against Arsenal at Highbury on 22 August 1999, for all of eighteen seconds.

Mark Dempsey made his United debut in the European Cup Winners Cup against Spartak Varna in November 1983, but had to wait a further two years before making his United league debut, against Ipswich Town in December 1985.

On the international front, Tommy Bogan, a United player between 1949 and 1951, must have the shortest career ever, not taking substitute appearances into account.

Playing for Scotland against England in April 1945, Bogan was injured within a minute of the start when he twisted his knee in a collision with England goalkeeper Frank Swift, forcing him to leave the field. He was never selected for his country again.

LIKE FATHER
LIKE SON

There are a number of family connections scattered through the history of Manchester United. Darren Ferguson had much to prove at Old Trafford under his father and was to make a total of 30 appearances between seasons 1990-91 and 1993-94. He is not, however, the only son of a United manager to play for the club, although he is the only one to play at first team level.

Jimmy Murphy's son Nick did come close on a couple of occasions, being named as substitute against Liverpool on 12 October 1968 and against Sunderland on 18 January 1969, while the current Academy manager Paul McGuinness failed to follow in his father Wilf's footsteps in the 1980s, only managing to make reserve team level.

Tommy Docherty's son Peter, played in the 1982 FA Youth Cup final, while assistant manager's Pat Crerand and Tommy Cavanagh both had son's in the junior sides.

Coach John Aston was perhaps the proudest father of all, watching his son, also named John, work his way through the United ranks, going on to win both a League championship medal and a European Cup winners medal during his time at Old Trafford.

Matt Busby's son Sandy was also a footballer, but did not play for United, only against them, at reserve team level for Blackburn Rovers.

BROTHERS
IN ARMS

The da Silva brothers are certainly the first set of twins to play together in the Manchester United first team, but they are far from being the first brothers to do so.

Gary and Phil Neville played together numerous times before Phil left for Goodison Park in 2005, while Jimmy and Brian Greenhoff made 80 appearances together between November 1976 and May 1979.

Martin and George Buchan shared a dressing room on only two occasions in September and October 1973, but prior to that you have to go right back to 27 December 1913, when James and John Hodge took the field together against Sheffield Wednesday for what was their only game side by side.

Fred and Harry Erentz managed four games together in season 1897-98, while Roger and Jack Doughty played 26 times together during 1889-90.

There have of course been other brothers at the club David and James Bain (1922-23 to 1923-24) and (1922-23 to 1927-28). David and Thomas Fitzsimmons (1895-96) and (1892-93 to 1893-94). James and John Hodge (1910-11 to 1918-19) and (1913-14 to 1918-19) and George and John Owen (1889-90) and (1887-88 to 1892-93), but none of those ever played at first team level together.

The Greenhoff brothers, on 28 October 1978 and the Doughty brothers, on 7 April 1890 are the only brothers to have scored in the same game.

As something of a postscript, if you want to include war-time fixtures, then you can throw Jack and Arthur Rowley into the mix, as they both played together between

1941-42 and 1943-44. Arthur was never to appear for the club outside of those wartime years, but made a name for himself as a noted goal scorer with West Bromwich Albion, Fulham, Leicester City and Shrewsbury Town with a record 434 in 619 league games.

KEEPING
RECORDS

Edwin Van der Sar joined Manchester United from Fulham in the summer of 2005 for a reported transfer fee of £2m and went on to set a number of individual records during his 266 games at the club.

When he won his fourth Premier League medal, he was aged 40 years and 205 days, becoming the oldest player ever to do so and the first non-British player to play in the Premier League over the age of 40.

He was also the second oldest player ever to play in a Champions League Final at the age of 40 years and 211 days, when he played in the 2011 Final against Barcelona. He was also the first goalkeeper to keep 50 clean sheets in the Champions League.

On 4 March 2009, he conceded a 9th minute goal against Newcastle United, bringing to an end a clean sheet record that had lasted 1,311 minutes, a world record.

His 130 caps for the Dutch national side is also a record for the Netherlands.

Edwin Van der Sar was not however the oldest player to play for Manchester United and would have to have played for a few more years to achieve that distinction.

Although not qualifying for a bus pass, the oldest player to represent United was legendary Welshman Billy Meredith, who was 46 years and 281 days when he took the field for a First Division fixture against Derby County on 7 May 1921. This was almost eight years older than the next oldest player Ryan Giggs who was 39 years and 171 days old at the end of this season (2012-13).

Billy Meredith's career did not however end at 46 with that ninety minutes against Derby County, as he re-joined his previous club Manchester City, playing in the semi-final of the FA Cup in 1924 against Newcastle United. His final match for City, at the ripe old age of 49 years and 245 days.

United's oldest post-war player prior to Ryan Giggs was Jack Warner, who played against Newcastle United on 22 April 1950 at the age of 38 years and 213 days.

MORE MEDALS
THAN AN ARMY

Ryan Giggs, is by far Manchester United's most decorated player with an enviable array of trophies.

The Welshman, who made his 1000th appearance for United, Wales and Great Britain during the 2012-13 season, has won 13 Premier League titles; four FA Cup winner's medals; four League Cup winner's medals; eight FA Community Shield plaques; two Champions league winner's medals; one UEFA Super Cup winner's medal; one Inter-Continental Cup winners medal and one FIFA Club World Cup winners medal in 2008.

There have also been countless individual awards such as *PFA Young Player of the Year* in 1991-92 and 1992-93, *PFA Players Player of the Year* in 2008-09, *BBC Sports Personality of the Year* in 2009 and the goal of the season in 1998-99 for that memorable strike against Arsenal in the FA Cup semi-final at Villa Park.

He has also scored in every season of the Premier League, as well as having scored United's quickest goal on record against Southampton on 18 November 1995, after only fifteen seconds.

It is interesting to note that Ryan's first appearances at Old Trafford, for England and Salford schools was under the name Ryan Wilson. When his parents split up a number of years later, he took his mother's maiden name.

And following David Moyes brief reign as manager in 2013-14, Giggs was also interim manager for the last few games of the season, making his final appearance as a substitute in the last game of the campaign.

STEP FORWARD
SIR BOBBY CHARLTON

FACT 29

Bobby Charlton won three FA Youth Cup winners medals, in 1954, 1955 and 1956, before making his first team debut against Charlton Athletic in October 1956, scoring twice in a 4-2 win. He survived the Munich disaster in 1958, going on to help England, with whom he won 106 caps, win the World Cup in 1966.

With United he had FA Cup and League Championship success, before scoring twice and captaining United to their European Cup Final victory in 1968.

Well known for his long ranged goals, not to mention his famous 'comb-over', it is hard to believe that in season 1972-73, he was United's leading scorer with a mere six goals.

Respected the world over, he was knighted for his services to football in June 1994. He is a director of the football club he served with distinction, making over 750 appearances and scoring over 240 goals between his debut in 1956 and his final game against Chelsea on 28 April 1973.

Following his retirement, he became player manager of Preston North End, but resigned two years later. A brief stint in Ireland, as a player with Waterford followed, as did an equally brief spell as caretaker manager of Wigan Athletic in 1976, where he was a director.

He was knighted for his services to the game in 1994.

STUMPED BY
BUSBY'S GARDEN WALL

Gorton born Roger Byrne made his United debut against Liverpool at Anfield in November 1951. He was capped 33 times by England between 1954 and 1957, with all his appearances coming in consecutive fixtures.

Although a full back, he featured in the United championship winning side of 1951-52 at outside left, scoring 7 goals, but never found the net at international level. He did, however, miss penalties against Brazil and Yugoslavia in 1956.

The United captain, who lost his life in the Munich air disaster also had the distinction of crashing his car into Matt Busby's garden wall one morning whilst heading to training. Byrne was uninjured in the accident and was given a lift to training by his surprised manager.

Byrne signed for United from the local Ryder Brow Youth Club and was also a keen cricketer. One of his team mates in the Ryder Brow team was Brian Statham, who went on to create his own success story, but as a cricketer, representing Lancashire and playing in 70 Test Matches for England.

Although good enough to represent Manchester United and England, Roger Byrne, who joined the RAF to do his national service, was not considered good enough to play for the football team where he was stationed!

YOUNGEST SIDE
TO TAKE THE FIELD

Manchester United is well known for bringing talented youngsters through the junior and reserve sides and into the first team.

Over the years there have been countless teenagers make that step up, but there have always been experienced professionals to guide them through those sometimes harrowing initial fixtures.

But back on 27 August 1955, what is regarded as the youngest United side to play in a League fixture took the field. The line-up of Ray Wood, Bill Foulkes, Roger Byrne, Jeff Whitefoot, Mark Jones, Duncan Edwards, Colin Webster, Jackie Blanchflower, Eddie Lewis, Dennis Viollet and Albert Scanlon made the average age of the team 22 years and 106 days.

In October 1960, against Bolton Wanderers, the team of Gregg, Setters, Brennan, Stiles, Foulkes, Nicholson, Moir, Giles, Dawson, Charlton and Scanlon were just ten days older.

The majority of the players in both those sides went on to enjoy lengthy careers with United, with those who didn't establishing themselves at other clubs.

WHAT'S IN
A NAME?

The modern day trend of the players having their names on the backs of their shirts helps the unfamiliar identify who they are actually watching, whilst also being something of a money spinner in the club souvenir shop.

However, it is perhaps fortunate that it is only a players surname that appears on the back of the shirts. Particularly in the case of the United player with the longest name, that of Dutch international midfielder from the 1980s - Arnoldus Johannus Hyacinthus Muhern.

The Dutchman only edging out Caesar Augustus Llewelyn Jenkyns, a noted individual who graced the Newton Heath stage during 1896-97.

As for the shortest name of a United player, you can take your pick of either Ian Ure or Tom Hay. However, for the latter, he was of course Thomas Hay, while Ure, the former Arsenal centre-half was christened John Francombe Ure.

So, then you would have to go for John Dow. Who mentioned Nani?

THE SAD CASE
OF TOMMY BLACKSTOCK

Former Liverpool manager Bill Shankly once said: "Some people believe football is a matter of life and death, I am very disappointed with that attitude. I can assure you it is much, much more important than that."

Sadly, in the case of United player Tommy Blackstock football actually cost him his life.

While playing in a Lancashire Combination fixture against St Helens Rec. in April 1907, with the game only ten minutes old, Blackstock jumped and headed the ball out of play for a throw in and immediately collapsed to the ground.

Following attention from the trainer, he was carried from the pitch, but before he could be taken to hospital, he died in the dressing room.

Following an inquest, it was announced that he had died from natural causes.

When his body was taken to the railway station to be transported to his native Kirkcaldy, his coffin was escorted there by his United team mates and club officials, with a considerable number of supporters also there to pay their final respects.

THE ONLY
WAY IS UP

It is often said that, as a player, after leaving United, there is only one way that you can go and that is down. This is not entirely correct, as one or two of names spring to mind who failed to make the grade with United, but went on to enjoy extended careers elsewhere.

David Platt, currently a first team coach at Manchester's 'other' club, left United in 1984, joining Crewe Alexandra, before going on to fame and fortune with the likes of Aston Villa, Bari, Juventus, Sampdoria, Arsenal, Nottingham Forest and England, playing over 500 games, scoring over 170 goals.

Not so well known is Alan McLaughlin, who left United two years after David Platt, but went on to make 42 appearances for the Republic of Ireland while playing with the likes of Portsmouth and Swindon Town.

Peter O'Sullivan was another who failed to make a first team appearance with United, but after leaving Old Trafford in 1970, he made over 400 appearances with Brighton and Hove Albion, winning 3 Welsh international caps.

UNITED'S MOST LOYAL SERVANT

Ryan Giggs joined Manchester United in 1987, making his debut in 1990 giving him a first team career of 24 years, far out stripping the next longest, Jack Rowley, who can only mange a mere 17 years and 98 days by comparison.

Neither, however, are able to match the consistency of Steve Coppell or Allenby Chilton.

Chilton was a first team regular for three consecutive seasons – 1951-52, 1952-53 and 1953-54. This record is bettered only by Steve Coppell, who made 206 consecutive appearances for the club between 13 January 1977 and 7 November 1981. A record that it is safe to say will never be beaten.

But if you simply want an example of club loyalty, then look no further than Les Olive. Joining United from school in 1942, Olive played as an amateur for United through the junior ranks to the first team, making two First Division appearances as an emergency goalkeeper during season 1952-53. He went on to become assistant secretary, stepping into the vacant office following the Munich disaster, retiring in 1988, then to take up a seat on the United board of directors, a position he held until 2005, a career that stretched some 63 years.

OFF IN
A FLASH

Sending's off can influence the outcome of any game, as United know only too well. But one Saturday afternoon many in the 20,409 crowd at Southampton were still getting to their places when the referee sent-off United's Liam O'Brien, for a foul, after only 85 seconds. This is the quickest ever dismissal in the top flight.

Making his debut for United in a League Cup tie against York City at Old Trafford on 20 September 1995, Pat McGibbon was sent off in the 51st minute, as United lost this Second round first leg tie 3-0. Irishman McGibbon never featured in another first team game for the club.

United also have the distinction of being the first club to have a player sent off in both an FA Cup final and a League Cup final.

In the 1985 FA Cup final, Kevin Moran was sent off for up-ending Everton's Peter Reid. Thankfully, although down to ten men, United still went on to lift the trophy thanks to a Norman Whiteside goal.

The 1994 Football League Cup final saw Andrie Kanchelskis sent off for hand ball on the goal line in the final minute. United lost 3-1.

Manchester United's first venture into FA Cup proved to be something of a disaster.

Whilst still known as Newton Heath, they were drawn away in the First Round, against Fleetwood Town, travelling to the Lancashire port on 30 October 1886 and taking a 1-0 lead, but by the end of the game were held at 2-2.

Expecting a replay on their own ground and with a train to catch back to Manchester, the Heathens were shocked to be told by the referee that they would be required to play thirty minutes extra time.

After much debate, the visitors stood by their initial decision of demanding a replay but to no avail and as they refused to play extra time, the referee had little alternative but to award the game to Fleetwood Town with the railway workers going out of the cup without having actually been defeated.

Their first victory in the competition came in October 1890, when they defeated Higher Walton at North Road 2-0. This fixture should have been played at Higher Walton, but they agreed to switch to Manchester in order to obtain better gate receipts.

OVER 100 YEARS ON, UNITED SHUN THE FA CUP FOR A SECOND TIME

Refusing to play in that 1886 FA Cup replay was not the only time that Manchester United were to turn their back on the competition, as following their treble success in 1999, the club was invited to play in the FIFA Club World Championship in Brazil, which was unfortunately scheduled for the last two weeks in January 2000.

United were under pressure from the government and the Football Association, due to the fact that both parties were keen to keep in favour with FIFA, as they wanted to be considered as hosts for the 2006 World Cup.

Despite numerous suggestions as how the club could compete in both competitions, United withdrew from the 1999-2000 FA Cup, becoming the first side not to defend the trophy. A strange decision really, as the Third Round of that season's competition was played in December and they could easily have been knocked out at this early stage, or even if they had won, fielded a team of reserve players.

But withdraw they did and as it turned out, United failed not only to win the World Club tournament, but failed to even reach the semi-finals after drawing with Necaxa 1-1 and losing to Vasco da Gama 3-1.

England was also ironically turned down for the 2006 World Cup!

United eventually did win the world crown in 2008, becoming the first British side to do so, when they beat LDU Quito1-0 in Yokohama, Japan on 21 December 2008.

ALL AWAY
TO WEMBLEY

When United won the FA Cup in season 1947-48, they played every tie away from home.

In the Third Round they were drawn away at Aston Villa, winning 6-4, which earned them a home draw with Liverpool in Round Four. But they were ground sharing with neighbours City at the time, due to war damage at Old Trafford. To further confound matters, City were also drawn at home, so it was agreed that the tie would be played at Goodison Park.

Despite something of 'home' advantage to their opponents, United progressed with a 3-0 win.

Round Five brought another home draw, with Charlton Athletic in opposition, but with City again having first option on Maine Road, United were again forced to play away and took the tie to Leeds Road, Huddersfield.

A 2-0 win put them in the quarter-finals, producing yet another home draw, but this time they could use Maine Road as City were no longer involved in the competition. Preston North End were no match for United, losing 4-1 and with the semi-finals played on neutral grounds, United were once again on the road, facing Derby County at Hillsborough, Sheffield, where they won 3-1.

The Final was of course at Wembley where, in one of the best ever finals, United overcame Blackpool 4-2 to win their first post-war honour and tier first under Matt Busby.

A FIRST FOR KNOWLEDGE

Over the years, Manchester United has claimed numerous 'firsts' – first English side to enter the European Cup and the first to win it. The first side to win the Premier League, first team to win the treble – Premier League, FA Cup and European Cup, first team to win the FA Charity Shield, first team to field three winners of the European Footballer of the Year in the same team.

The first team in the world to have their own dedicated television channel, with MUTV launched on 10 September 1998 and numerous other footballing firsts. But one that tends to be forgotten about is that they were the first club to claim 'third place' in the FA Cup.

Season 1969-70 saw the Football Association decide on what they hoped would be a money making venture, by creating a 'third Place play-off' fixture between the two beaten semi-finalists, who in that particular season were United and Watford.

Played on the eve of the cup final, another ploy, so that many FA members could attend, the game at Arsenal's Highbury stadium attracted a mere 15,105 spectators as United beat Watford 2-0 with two Brian Kidd goals.

Due to lack of interest, this particular fixture was to last only for a further four seasons before being confined to the history books.

Ironically Old Trafford was where the 69-70 winners Chelsea actually lifted the cup. Following a draw in the Wembley final against Leeds who had knocked United out, the pitch was in such a terrible state that the Football Association decided to play the replay at United's ground.

WATCHING ON THE
TV AT OLD TRAFFORD

The first ever First Division Football League game to be shown live via closed circuit television was beamed to Old Trafford from Arsenal's Highbury stadium on Friday 3 March 1967.

A crowd of 63,363 witnessed the 1-1 draw unfold live in London, while 28,423, equally vocal and enthusiastic supporters watched the fixture on large screens, situated on the Old Trafford pitch.

On 23 April 1969, the European Cup semi-final first leg 2-0 defeat against AC Milan was screened live from Italy, with 22,500 present on this occasion

United's 'home' leg of their European Cup Winners Cup tie against St Etienne was switched to Plymouth following crowd trouble in the first leg in France, and attracted 27,245 to watch it at Old Trafford on 5 October 1977.

The 1990s also saw various Premier League fixtures screened live to the ground.

42

UNITED AND LIVERPOOL
IN COLLUSION

On Good Friday 1915, the 18,000 at Old Trafford had every reason to think that something was just not quite right. United were battling against relegation, but had a two goal advantage over a strong Liverpool side.

Pagnam of Liverpool was spoken to by team mates after hitting the United bar with a shot. The visitors also missed a penalty and after the match, even the referee said that he felt something was not quite right.

Following the game, rumblings began to be heard regarding the match being fixed. So much so, that the Football Association ordered a hearing into the events. As it turned out there had been a meeting between players of both sides, a few days prior to the game in the nearby Dog and Partridge Hotel, which had seen them agree to fix the score line at 2-0 in United's favour.

The eventuality was that Sandy Turnbull, Arthur Whalley and Enoch West of United and four Liverpool players were banned for life.

The bans were lifted on all but West and Turnbull after the First World War, the latter having died during the hostilities. West fought until 1945 to have the ban lifted.

It is interesting to note that Tommy Miller, one of the Liverpool players actually signed for United after the lifting of the ban, while another of those Liverpool players was Jackie Sheldon, who had been a United player prior to joining the Merseyside club.

United, by the way, finished the season one point ahead of second bottom Chelsea and two ahead of bottom club Tottenham Hotspur.

43
TITLE RETAINED
IN STYLE

As United attempted to retain their Premier League title in season 1998-99, they travelled to Nottingham Forest's City Ground on Saturday 6 February 1999, having just appointed Steve McLaren as assistant manager. The 30,025 in the ground witnessed something of a remarkable feat in goal scoring.

United opened the scoring as early as the 2nd minute through Dwight Yorke, but Forest equalised four minutes later. Andy Cole made it 2-1 in the 7th minute and that was it until five minutes into the second half when the same player increased United's lead.

Yorke made it 4-1 in the 67th minute and with the game more or less won, Alex Ferguson sent on Ole Gunnar Solskjær in the 72nd minute to replace Dwight Yorke.

With 10 minutes remaining, and the score still 4-1, the United substitute increased United's lead and went on to score a further three goals before full time, giving United an 8-1 victory and what is still the highest recorded away win in the Premier League and also the first time that a substitute has scored four goals in a game.

It also believed that the nine goal thriller created something of another record, as only ten shots were on target from either side during those ninety minutes, giving a 90% shots on target ratio.

MOMENTS OF
MIXED FORTUNES

There have been a number of astonishing reversals, results wise, throughout United's history. Some have brought sweet revenge, others simply a mirror image of the previous fixture.

On 31 December 1892, Newton Heath ran out 1-7 winners against Derby County at home in a First Division fixture, only to lose 7-1 at Stoke a week later on 7 January 1893. The Heathens team for both games would have been identical had it not been for the absence of goalkeeper Warner. He failed to turn up at Stoke, having missed the train, forcing Stewart to play in goal and the visitors to play with only 10 men.

In the 1897-98 season, Woolwich Arsenal defeated Newton Heath 5-1 in London on 8 January, only to lose 5-1 in the return fixture in Manchester on 26 February.

A 3-2 Christmas Day 1931 victory over Wolverhampton Wanderers in a Division Two fixture saw a complete reversal the following day when they lost 7-0. An even stranger Christmas reversal came in 1963, when United lost 6-1 at Burnley on Boxing Day, but two days later, after making two changes, saw Burnley defeated 5-1 at Old Trafford.

In October 1965, United lost 5-1 to Spurs at White Hart Lane, but in the Old Trafford return fixture in December, United gained their revenge with a 5-1 win.

THE GREATEST COMEBACK
=
FACT 45 THE GREATEST PRIZE

Well known for their comebacks, United have shocked many sides, as well as their own supporters, with some dramatic fight backs. None, however, can match that of 26 May 1999, when losing 1-0 to the German's of Bayern Munich in the Champions League final in Barcelona, two goals in stoppage time from Teddy Sheringham and Ole Gunnar Solskjær plucked the trophy from their opponents grasp to give them an unprecedented treble.

Other notable comebacks are – 12 February 1910 when losing 3-0 at St James Park Newcastle, United turned it around to win 4-3. Against Tottenham Hotspur at White Hart Lane in September 2001, United found themselves 3-0 behind and humiliated at half time. The second forty-five minutes turned out to be a completely different story, as United turned the game around, not simply drawing level, but going on to win 5-3.

Although ninety minutes gives you much more time to turn a game around than forty-five, United's European Cup Winners Cup quarter final second leg victory over Barcelona

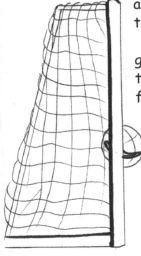
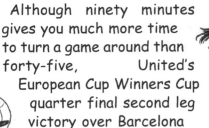

at Old Trafford in 1984, is a comeback up there with the best.

2-0 down from the first leg at the Nou Camp, two goals from Bryan Robson and one from Frank Stapleton, turned the game on its head and United went through 3-2 on aggregate in front of a packed 58,547 Old Trafford.

Returning to that memorable 1998-99 season, 1-0 down against fierce rivals Liverpool in the FA Cup fourth round tie at Old Trafford, Dwight Yorke pulled a goal back in the 88th minute, leaving a replay at Anfield looming before Ole Gunnar Solskjær popped up for a Nou Camp dress rehearsal with a last gasp winner.

One final dramatic finale, this time from April 2009. 2-1 down to Aston Villa at home and the title looking as if it would slip from United's grasp. With ten minutes remaining, Ronaldo equalised, but no matter how hard they tried, it just did not look as if a goal would materialise. Then three minutes into the five minutes of added time, substitute Macheda somehow lost his marker, turned and curled the ball wide of Friedal and into the far corner. Heart stopping moments indeed.

DOING IT
THE HARD WAY

Winning the Champions League in season 1998-99 was no simple straight forward business, as United had to begin their march to glory in the Second Qualifying Round, where they defeated FC Lodz 2-0 at home, drawing the away second leg 0-0.

Placed in 'Group D', where they were paired with Bayern Munich, Barcelona and Brondby, they drew their first two fixtures, 3-3 at Old Trafford against Barcelona and 2-2 in Munich, before thumping Brondby 6-2 in Copenhagen and 5-0 at Old Trafford. Barcelona were again held to a 3-3 draw, as were the German's at Old Trafford, 1-1. A result that gave United second place in their group.

In the quarter finals they defeated Inter Milan 2-0 at home, a victory that was enough to see them through, as they drew the second leg 1-1 in Italy. The semi-finals also saw Italian opposition, with Juventus snatching what was considered an important away goal in the 1-1 draw in Manchester, but in the second leg United won by the odd goal in five, sending them into the Final in Barcelona.

On a memorable may evening, it was not until the 1st and 3rd minutes of stoppage time that United clinched the trophy, with goals from Sheringham and Solskjær.

It was estimated that over 500,000 packed the streets of Manchester the following day to see the team parade through the city centre in an open top bus.

EUROPEAN TOUR
SETS RECORD
IN HUNGARY

Champions League football and friendly fixtures scattered across the globe are a regular feature on the Manchester United fixture list these days, but they are all a far cry from their first pioneering overseas adventure in May 1908.

As a reward for winning the club's first League title, the team were taken on a nine game tour, playing in Vienna, Prague and Budapest. The second last of those nine fixtures was a 7-0 victory against Ferencvaros, in front of a 12,000 crowd, the highest ever recorded in Hungary at that time.

However the United players were attacked during the game, coming under a hail of stones and other objects, as the referee tried to send off three United players for an infringement of the rules. After much debate, they were allowed to remain on the pitch, but they did have to be rescued by mounted police and were later subjected to another attack by supporters of the home club before returning safely to their hotel.

The tour was completed undefeated.

NO TURKISH DELIGHT
FOR THE RED DEVILS

FACT 48

When Turkish side Galatasaray held United to a 3-3 draw at Old Trafford on 20 October 1993, this brought to an end a sequence of seventeen successive home victories in Europe, stretching back to September 1957.

Another Turkish club, Fernerbache were to bring to an end United's unbeaten home European run, when they surprisingly won 1-0 in October 1996, bringing to an end a record that encompassed some fifty-seven fixtures and covered more than forty years.

Strangely, having seen their long and successful run come to an end, United were to lose two of

their following three home fixtures in European competition.

EUROPEAN COMPETITION CLOSE TO HOME

European football offers clubs the opportunity to compete against the best continental club sides, but from time to time the draw has thrown together clubs from the same domestic league.

In the case of Manchester United, they have found themselves paired with other English clubs on a few occasions, having met Chelsea and Arsenal in the Champions League, Tottenham Hotspur in the old European Cup Winners Cup and Everton in the older Inter Cities Fairs Cup.

There have also been meetings with Scottish sides in Europe, facing both of the Glasgow clubs, Rangers and Celtic in the Champions League and Dundee United in the UEFA Cup (what was the old Inter Cities Fairs Cup).

They have faced one Welsh side, Wrexham in the European Cup Winners Cup and Irish sides Shamrock Rovers and Waterford in the European Cup.

THE FIRST
EUROPEAN SUCCESS

Manchester United became the first English club to win the European Cup in 1968, beating Hibernians of Malta 4-0 on aggregate in Round One, Sarajevo 2-1 on aggregate in the Second Round, Gornik Zabrze 2-1 on aggregate in the quarter-finals and Real Madrid 4-3 on aggregate in the semi-finals before the 4-1 extra time victory over Benfica in the Final at Wembley.

Strangely though, United failed to win any of their away legs, drawing 0-0 in Malta, 0-0 in Sarajevo, losing 1-0 in Poland and drawing 3-3 in Madrid.

United used only fourteen players during their cup run, with Shay Brennan only making two appearances, in the semi-final second leg and the final.

Reserve team goalkeeper Jimmy Rimmer was substitute in the final, as clubs were allowed to name only a substitute 'keeper.

Brian Kidd scored in the final on what was his nineteenth birthday.

THE TRIP TO ITALY THAT TOOK A WEEK

World-wide travel is easy today with regular flights around the globe, with a couple of hours taking you from a rain drenched Britain to the Mediterranean sun. But back in those early days of European football, and in particular following the Munich air disaster, Manchester United found things far from easy or straight forward.

With the horrors of Munich still very much in everyone's mind and with a European cup semi-final tie against AC Milan, the club decided upon something of a long haul in order to fulfil their commitments.

Few within the club wanted to fly again so soon after the crash, so the club decided to travel by train and boat, but it was to be a long and drawn out journey, leaving Manchester's London Road station at 200 pm on Saturday May 10th and not arriving in Milan until 8.20 am on Monday May 12th. This did include an overnight stop in London.

The journey home was equally as long, more so perhaps following the 4-0 defeat, as they left Milan on Friday May 16th at 5.22pm, arriving back at London Road at 9.40pm on the 17th.

HAT-TRICK
HEROS

The club's first hat-trick was scored by William Stewart against Small Heath on 7 April 1890, in a 9-1 Football Alliance victory. Stewart also scored in the club's first Alliance match against Sunderland at the start of that same season.

The quickest hat-trick, however, is debatable, as Ernie Goldthorpe is reported as scoring three between the 62nd and 66th minute of United's match against Notts County at Old Trafford on 10 February 1923, while Ole Gunnar Solskjær claimed a hat trick against Nottingham Forest at the City Ground in the final five minutes of the game on 6 February 1999.

Charlie Mitten claimed a hat trick of penalties against Aston Villa on 8 March 1950, in United's 7-0 victory, apparently telling the unfortunate Villa goalkeeper where he was going to place each one.

But the most unusual hat trick ever scored by a United player was at Old Trafford on 26 November 1966, when David Herd scored three in United's 5-0 win over Sunderland, his goals coming against three different goalkeepers.

His first against Sunderland's usual custodian Jim Montgomery, but he received an injury and was replaced by outfield player Charlie Hurley, who was in turn replaced at half time by John Parke. None could stop Herd.

THE GOAL
SCORING DEBUTS

A number of players have marked their Manchester United debut with a goal, with Harold Halse recording the quickest, scoring after only thirty seconds against Sheffield Wednesday on 28 March 1908.

Alex Dawson went two steps better than Halse, scoring on his debut in three different competitions. Against Burnley in the First Division on 22 April 1957, his FA Cup debut against Sheffield Wednesday on 19 February 1958 and against Exeter City in the League Cup on 19 October 1960.

This is arguably bettered by David Herd, who scored in his first game in five different cup competitions – the FA Cup, Football League Cup, European Cup, European Cup Winners Cup and the Inter Cities Fairs Cup. He failed, however, to score on his League debut, but did actually score on his United debut, a friendly against Bayern Munich on 9 August 1961.

Ole Gunnar Solskjær became the first United substitute to score on his debut, against Blackburn Rovers on August 1996, but Charlie Sagar, on 2 September 1905, against Bristol City on the opening day of the season and Wayne Rooney against Fenerbache on 28 September 2004, are the only United player's to score a hat trick on their debuts.

Tommy Reid, William Brooks, Jack Allen, George Livingstone, George Nicholl, Tommy Taylor, Bobby Charlton, Shay Brennan and Paul Scholes have all scored twice on their United debuts.

On 15 September 2012 Alexander Buttner and Nick Powell both scored on their United debut against Wigan Athletic at Old Trafford., the only time two players have scored on their United debuts.

Goals are what the supporters pay their admission money for and over the years, United have given better value than most. Their record score lines in the major competitions are as follows –

Football League –
10-1 v Wolverhampton Wanderers,
15 October 1892, North Road, Manchester.
Premier League –
9-0 v Ipswich Town, 4 March 1995, Old Trafford.
FA Cup –
8-0 v Yeovil Town, Fifth Round, 12 February 1949,
Maine Road, Manchester.
League Cup –
7-2 v Newcastle United, Fourth Round,
17 October 1976, Old Trafford.
Charity Shield –
8-4 v Swindon Town,
25 September 1911, Stamford Bridge.
European Cup –
10-0 v Anderlecht, preliminary round,
26 September 1956, Maine Road, Manchester.
Champions League –
7-1 v Roma, quarter final, 10 April 2007, Old Trafford.
UEFA Cup/Fairs Cup –
6-1 v Djurgardens, First round second leg,
27 October 1964, Old Trafford.
6-1 v Borussia Dortmund, Second Round,
First leg, 11 November 1964, Rote Erde Stadion.
Cup Winners Cup –
6-1 v Willem, First Round, Second leg,
15 October 1963, Old Trafford.

NOT TO BE DWELLED ON - THE HEAVIEST DEFEATS

There have also been occasions when the glut of goals have not gone in United's favour, with a few of their heaviest defeats being –

0-7 v Blackburn Rovers (A) 10 April 1926; v Aston Villa (A) 27 December 1930; v Wolves (A) 26 December 1931.

0-6 v Aston Villa (H) 14 March 1914; v Huddersfield Town (H) 10 September 1930; v Leicester City (A) 21 January 1961; v Ipswich Town (A) 1 March 1980.

1-7 v Burnley FA Cup (A) 13 February 1901; v Newcastle United (H) 10 September 1927.

2-7 v Sheffield Wednesday FA Cup (H) 1 February 1961.

There are obviously more, but we do not want to dwell on such results, particularly against certain teams!

THE RECORD
ATTENDANCES

Although Old Trafford today holds some 75,000 spectators, the highest Football League attendance ever to watch a Manchester United home fixture was recorded as 81,962 against Arsenal on 17 January 1948.

However, that particular fixture was not played at Old Trafford, but at Manchester City's Maine Road ground where United were rent paying lodgers until season 1949-50. This was due to their own home beside the Ship Canal having been partly destroyed by German bombs on the evening of 11 March 1941 during an air raid on the nearby industrial area of Trafford Park.

There is also some debate as to how exact the attendance for that Arsenal fixture really is, with 83,260 being considered as nearer to the number of people inside Maine Road that afternoon.

The attendance for that particular fixture against Arsenal was surpassed, however, twelve months later when a massive 82,771 clicked through the turnstiles to watch United play Bradford Park Avenue in a Fourth Round FA Cup tie, a game that ended 1-1.

Rather ironically, the game that drew the largest attendance at Old Trafford, prior to the modern day ground developments, did not involve United, with 76,962 present to watch the FA Cup semi-final between Wolverhampton Wanderers and Grimsby Town in March 1939.

THE PRICE
OF LOYAL DEVOTION

FACT 57

Season tickets for Old Trafford were, at one point, akin to some family artefact, an item tenderly looked after over the years and handed down through the generations. Few became available to the general public, with a waiting list which would compare to a good crowd for a lower division fixture.

Today they are more readily obtainable, at a price, with the waiting list no more. But what is that price and how has it changed over the years?

If you go back to 1902-03 the stand at the Bank Street ground was roofed for the first time and it could accommodate 8,000 spectators. In the *Athletic News* at the start of that season, it mentions that "guinea members are to have quite an ideal position". Those members would be the early 'season ticket holders', as the board were well aware that due to times being hard, this was a way of getting money in the bank, by having the public pay for games before they were played.

Move forward some 24 years and a season ticket for the 'Ladies Chairs' in the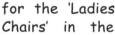

 main stand at Old Trafford would have cost the sum of £2 2/- (£2.10p), while ten years later to 1936-37 and a 'Gents Ground' season ticket carried the pricey figure of £1.

Post war, a 'Reserved Enclosure' stand seat for season 1949-50 was £5 5/- (£5.25p), with a seat in 'B Stand' in 1954-55 priced at £6.10/- (£6.50p). By season 1961-62, 'Stand C' seasons tickets were priced at £8 10/- (£8.50p), with a seat in 'Stand B' to watch United lift the championship in 1965-66 was priced at £10.

By now, there was also the cantilever stand along the United Road side of the ground and a 'G Stand' season ticket for 1969-70 on this side of the ground cost £9.

Suddenly, the prices were rising and for the Centenary season of 1978-79, your 'B Stand' seat was now £41, while over in 'H Stand' for 1985-86 it was up to £96.

Today, a seat in the Sir Alex Ferguson Stand tier 1 could put you back £950, with the cheapest season ticket, behind the goal at either end, considerably less, at £532.

NOT JUST THE HOME OF THE RED DEVILS

Old Trafford is known across the world as United's home but over the years it has also hosted much more than football.

Athletic meetings were held at the ground in the 1920s, while tennis legend Suzanne Lenglen, who won 31 Championship titles between 1914 and 1926, including 6 at Wimbledon, staged an exhibition there in 1927.

Baseball during the Second World War, floodlit cricket, Rugby League and Rugby Union have all graced the famous turf, as has boxing, when the WBC Super-Middleweight title fight between Nigel Benn and Chris Eubank was held there in October 1993.

It has also hosted various rock concerts, with acts such as Rod Stewart, Bon Jovi, Bruce Springsteen, Simply Red and Status Quo, having also kept the neighbours awake.

The BBC's *Songs of Praise* was also recorded there in September 1994.

THE SADDEST GATHERING
AT OLD TRAFFORD

On the evening of 10 February 1958, a large crowd gathered outside Old Trafford, but they were not there for ninety minutes of football.

There was little noise, except for muffled sobs, while the stadium stood in darkness. Many had stood for hours in the late evening rain, but this did little to deter them, as they were there to pay their final respects to Roger Byrne, Eddie Colman, Geoff Bent, Mark Jones, Tommy Taylor, Walter Crickmer, Bert Whalley, Tom Curry and journalists Alf Clarke and Tom Jackson, who had all lost their lives at Munich some four days previously.

They had gathered, awaiting the cortege that was bringing the bodies of those players, officials and journalists from Ringway airport, having been flown in from Munich earlier. Thousands lined the route, with any late night traffic coming to a standstill, as the coffins made their way to the Old Trafford gymnasium, where they would lie overnight before going their separate ways for burial and cremation.

THE LOWEST ATTENDANCES

The almost regular 70,000 odd spectators clicking through the Old Trafford turnstiles are the envy of every other Football League club, but there have been occasions when the click of the turnstiles has been barely audible.

On 2 September 1931, the smallest attendance for a Football League match at Old Trafford was recorded at 3,507 for a Second Division fixture against Southampton. Three days later, only 3,000 more turned up to watch United play Swansea Town.

Post war, the smallest attendance was for the 1952 FA Charity Shield fixture against Newcastle United on 24 September 1952 when only 11,381 bothered to turn up. The main reason for this was the 5.15 kick-off time.

The smallest post-war Football League crowd was a mere 11,968 for the visit of Fulham on the final day of the 1949-50 campaign.

But all those attendances are surpassed by what is considered to be the smallest crowd in Football League history – 13.

It came on 7 May 1921, an afternoon that saw Old Trafford host two consecutive games, United v Derby County and Stockport County v Leicester City. Crowd trouble at Stockport's Edgeley Park in their previous fixture had seen their ground closed and so they sought permission to play their final game of the season at Old Trafford.

10,000 watched United defeat the Ram's 3-0 and many stayed on to get two games for the price of one, but only thirteen actually paid to enter the ground after the United match. It is thought that perhaps between 1,000 and 2,000 watched the Stockport match.

THE BEST ATTENDED AWAY GAMES

"You've only come to see United" is a popular modern day chant. How many at a Manchester United away fixture actually turned up to see the opposition is not recorded, but it is fair to say that while they do attract the best away attendances for domestic fixtures, there will be a considerable number who were indeed, only there to see United.

The top five post-war United away attendances in the Football League and FA Cup are – 77,920 v Everton at Goodison Park; an FA Cup Fifth round tie on 14 February 1953. 74,723 at Maine Road for the Fourth round FA Cup tie against Manchester City on 29 January 1955. 72,077 for the First Division fixture against Everton at Goodison Park on 4 September 1957. 70,882 at White Hart Lane v Tottenham Hotspur on 22 September 1951 and 70,483 v Manchester City at Maine Road on 28 December 1957.

LIGHTING UP
OLD TRAFFORD

Due to there being no floodlights at Old Trafford prior to March 1957, Manchester United had to play the home legs of their first three European Cup ties, against the Belgian side Anderlecht, Borussia Dortmund, the German champions and the Spaniards of Athletic Bilbao at Manchester City's Maine Road ground.

Having finally erected floodlights, at the cost of £40,000, the first fixture played under them was the First Division match against Bolton Wanderers on 25 March 1957, when 60,862 saw United lose 2-0.

The first European Cup tie played under the new lights was a month later on 25 April against Real Madrid.

Erected on four tall pylons, three of which were situated outside the actual walls of the ground, they continued to be used until 1987 when, following the completion of the cantilever roof around to all four sides of the ground, they were dismantled and the new lights placed along the roof of the stands.

THE MUNICH MEMORIALS

The Munich Tunnel adds a poignant reminder to everyone of that bleak February day in Munich when eight Manchester United players were to lose their lives, along with club secretary Walter Crickmer, trainer Tom Curry, coach Bert Whalley and twelve others. The Munich clock is another reminder of that day in 1958, as is the nearby Munich Memorial.

Many who stop and stare at this memorial on the wall of the East stand will have no knowledge that this is in fact the fourth location of the plaque and certainly not the original one.

The original plaque was unveiled by manager Matt Busby on 25 February 1960 above what was the main entrance to the ground and where the director's entrance is today. It was similar to the one we see today and was worked from solid quartzite, enclosed by red Balmoral granite, which formed the perimeter wall of the scale model of the ground.

Two teak figures, a player and a spectator, stood on either side of a laurel leaf and a ball, which was inscribed 1958, flanked by two torches.

This memorial was lost when the south stand was developed, as it could not be removed and a new one, similar to the original was made and erected on the wall of K stand, where the Sir Matt Busby statue stands today.

It was then moved to the right hand side wall of K stand, before being moved again to its present site.

64

BRAZILLIAN LEGEND
IS THE OPENING ACT

The Manchester United Museum within the huge North Stand, is now one of the north-west's top tourist attractions It combines thousands of items of memorabilia, from Sandy Turnbull's 1909 FA Cup Final shirt, to a special treble winning exhibition some ninety years later. Along with programmes, photographs, medals, and even a stuffed goats head, it mixes the old with modern day interactive exhibits. As well as an audio guide available in nine different languages, unfolding the history of the club in front of your eyes.

Officially opened by Brazilian legend Pele in April 1998, it is a far cry from the original small, compact museum which was opened in 1986 and was the first of its kind in the world - situated in what was the Sir Matt Busby Suite, just off the main forecourt, underneath where the Munich clock is today.

United, as they have been in countless other fields, were the first club to have their own museum.

TRAFFIC CONGESTION AS OLD TRAFFORD OPENS ITS GATES FOR THE FIRST TIME

FACT **65**

The first match at Old Trafford took place on 19 February 1910, with Lancashire rivals Liverpool the opposition.

The official attendance for the fixture, which Liverpool won 4-3, is given as 50,000, but it is estimated that a further 5,000 gained free admission by various means due to some of the actual work not being completed.

All approaches to the ground were packed with traffic and pedestrians, with many of those in trams and taxis abandoning them and making their way on foot, eager not to miss any of the action.

Admission on the day was 6d (less than 3p) for the ground, with the covered (and only) stand costing 1/- (5p), 1/6d (less than 8p) and 2/- (10p). There were a few reserved seats at 5/- (25p).

As for the game itself, United were 2-0 in front within the opening fifteen minutes, Sandy Turnbull headed home the first goal at the new ground with its 'billiard table green turf', with Homer adding a second. Liverpool pulled a goal back, but United struck again through Wall. Much to the disappointment of the vast majority present, goals from Goddard and two from Stewart gave the visitors a 4-3 victory.

66
THE DAY OLD TRAFFORD LET FANS IN FOR FREE

Tickets for games at Old Trafford can be like gold dust, especially when it's an important cup tie, or the visitors are one of the club's big rivals. Outside the ground on those occasions, tickets can exchange hands for many times over face value on the illegal 'black market'.

On the afternoon of Wednesday 4 November 1981, however, there were no ticket touts, in fact there were no tickets or indeed an admission charge, as the gates at Old Trafford were thrown open to anyone who cared to come along and watch a United XI play Sydney Olympic in a friendly fixture.

The reason for the free admission was due to the fact that the United directors were unsure as to how many people would actually turn up for the 2pm kick-off, making the expense of employing gatemen something that might not be justified. Schoolmasters and employers were the only ones to complain and around 3,000 attended the match which United won 2-1.

THE THEATRE
OF ALIENS

FACT **67**

Attending a match can be an out of this world experience,

more so if it is your first visit to the stadium, perhaps rightly named 'The Theatre of Dreams'.

But on the evening of 31 October 1992, those present for the Premiership fixture against Wimbledon were, according to the American *National Enquirer* newspaper were confronted by more than twenty-two players kicking a ball.

Within the pages of one of its November editions it reported: *at a recent Manchester United home fixture, 47,000 fans were scared out of their wits and screamed in terror, when a UFO hovered above them. Within seconds, they were shrieking in panic and pointing to the sky. Players were running in a frantic daze, aware that they were being watched by aliens (!)*

A photographer had supplied the newspaper with four photographs and a supporter gave an eye witness account, but surprisingly (?) nothing appeared in the British press.

A fixture against Wimbledon at that time, however, could I suppose have produced anything!

THE PROTEST
THAT NEVER HAPPENED

In June 2005, the Glazer family took over control of
Manchester United sparking long running protests from a
number of supporters outside the stadium on a number of
occasions. Some of those protests were planned with
military precision, but these were not the first protests
planned for the ground.

Season 1930-31 was nothing short of disastrous,
with every one of the opening twelve fixtures being lost.
Attendances dropped from 18,004 on the opening day to
10,907 for the third home fixture, while score lines such
as the 6-2 defeat at Chelsea, the 6-0 defeat at home to
Huddersfield and the 7-4 defeat, again at home, to
Newcastle United , were not tolerated by the support and
it was soon obvious to everyone that frustration was
mounting.

By mid-October, things were reaching boiling point
and following the 5-1 defeat at West Ham, the Supporters
Club called a meeting at Hulme Town Hall on the night of
Friday 17 October, hours before the visit of Arsenal to
Old Trafford. Some 3,000 attended the meeting and the
board were unanimously given a vote of no confidence,
while Mr Greenhough, the Supporters club secretary,
proposed that the match the following day should be
boycotted.

So, armed with his soapbox, Mr Greenhough set off
for Old Trafford hoping that the feelings of the meeting
the previous night would be carried over and the board
would pay attention to the most important people behind
the club – its supporters.

Extra police were on duty outside the ground to quell

any unruly behaviour. Heavy rain seemed to dampen the spirits a little and the intended boycott was reported in the press as a failure, due to the attendance of 23,406. Not only the highest of the season to date, but the highest for the entire season, with the exception of the Manchester 'derby' against neighbours City, which attracted 39,876.

Many had travelled to the ground to view the pre-match events, expecting considerable excitement, but after listening to what Mr Greenhough had to say, they simply paid their admission money at the turnstiles and watched the game against Arsenal which United lost 2-1.

A DAY RETURN
TO THE SOUTH STAND
69

There are many different options open to the supporter of today on how to get to and from Old Trafford on a match-day. One of those is by barge, drifting along the canal from Manchester city centre, but a more popular mode of transport is by train, which is certainly convenient, dropping you off right outside the ground and if you sit in the South Stand, it is only a handful of steps to your seat.

When the ground was still in the planning stages, a station was something that architect Archibald Leitch had wanted to include, but he could not persuade the Cheshire Lines Railway to go along with his idea.

It was not until 1935, twenty-seven years later that the station was finally opened, running a direct service to Central Station (G-Mex).

Strangely, the railway company had a written agreement with the club guaranteeing them compensation against any loss.

THE THEATRE
OF NEUTRAL FIXTURES

Old Trafford has not simply played host to United's league, cup and friendly fixtures, as it has hosted internationals, neutral cup-ties, cup semi-finals and finals.

Among the internationals that have been played there are – England v Scotland 17 April 1926, England v Ireland 16 November 1938 and Hungary v Portugal 13 July 1966.

Neutral cup-ties – Liverpool v Preston North End FA Cup Fifth round, second replay 1962, Rochdale v Hartlepool United FA Cup first round, second replay 1958 and Barrow v Grimsby Town FA Cup first round, second replay 1964.

Semi-finals – Barnsley v Everton 1910 replay, Wolverhampton Wanderers v Cardiff City 1921 replay and Huddersfield Town v Sheffield United 1928.

The ground has hosted six finals – 26 April 1911 FA Cup replay between Bradford City and Newcastle United; 24 April 1915 FA Cup between Sheffield United and Chelsea; 11 April 1970 FA Cup replay between Chelsea and Leeds United (considered the roughest match ever played in England, despite no-one being sent off); 13 April 1977 League Cup second replay between Aston Villa and Everton; 22 March 1978 League Cup between Nottingham Forest and Liverpool, and on 28 May 2003 the Champions League final between Milan and Juventus.

FACT 71

SUMMERTIME BLUES FOR THE REDS

The month of June usually finds footballers enjoying a well-earned summer break, before returning to the rigours of pre-season training, with their season having come to an end around early to mid-May.

This however was not the case on two occasions, as the United players still found themselves in competitive action when all thoughts were normally taken up by holidays.

The first was on 1 June 1940, with United lining up at Old Trafford to play their final 'War Regional League – Western Region' fixture of the season against Everton.

Their season had begun on 26 August with a First Division fixture against Grimsby Town, but the Second World War brought an end to all

the domestic league's two weeks later, with regional Divisions taking over.

This fixture against Everton is the one and only time that United have played in a domestic competition in June. Not only is that in itself an oddity, but the United team on that afternoon is one for the connoisseurs, with the inclusion of football greats, such as Alec Herd (father of United's sixties star David), Peter Doherty, Raich Carter and the incomparable Stanley Matthews, all legendary figures from a bygone age. Arguably the most talented forward line ever to pull on the red shirt, but they still lost 3-0!

Some twenty-five years later, United once again found themselves playing in June, this time in the old Inter Cities Fairs Cup. Having reached the semi-finals, they were paired with Hungarian club Ferencvaros and in the first leg at Old Trafford on 31 May secured a 3-2 victory.

In the return leg played on 6 June, however, they were beaten 1-0, leaving it all square on aggregate. No extra time, no penalties, just a toss of the coin for the play-off venue, which United lost, so it was back to Hungary on 16 June, where United lost 2-1. This was nine months and twenty-six days since the start of that 1964-65 season.

THE DAY UNITED
NEARLY THREW THE MATCH

The laws of the game state that a goal cannot be scored direct from a throw in unless, that is, if it touches another player before entering the net. Such a scenario has occurred on just a very odd occasion and of course, if it was to happen then sure enough United would want in on the act.

At Oakwell on 22 January 1938, in the thirteenth minute of an FA Cup Fourth round tie against Barnsley at Oakwell, United were winning 1-0 thanks to a Johnny Carey goal two minutes earlier. The home side won a throw in near the corner flag. This was taken by Bokas, who had earned something of a reputation for being able to throw the ball some distance, with the Barnsley player launching the ball into the United penalty area.

Standing in the centre of his goal, Tommy Breen jumped for the ball, but only managed to get his finger tips to it, touching it into his own net. This was actually the first recorded goal scored in this manner.

Fortunately, United managed to secure an equaliser to spare their goalkeepers blushes.

Tommy Breen also had the unwanted distinction of being beaten within a minute of the kick-off of his debut against Leeds United at Elland Road in November 1936.

FIXTURES PILED
UP LIKE SNOW

Season 1962-63 saw the Football League and FA Cup programme devastated by the weather, as snow and ice covered the country.

Between December 26th, a 1-0 win at Fulham and February 23rd, a home match against Blackpool, the only games that United played were three friendly fixtures on deplorable pitches in Ireland against Bolton Wanderers, Coventry City and a Dublin X1.

Such was the backlog of fixtures, United played eight games in each of the months of March, April and May. Included in the March fixtures were fourth, fifth and sixth rounds of the FA Cup, played between the 11th and 30th of the month. Two league games were also played within that same period.

Strangely, the United players adapted well in the FA Cup, reaching the final where they defeated favourites Leicester City 3-1. In the First division, it was something of a different story, as they flirted with relegation and it was only a 1-1 draw at Maine Road, against fellow strugglers Manchester City that saved them from the drop into the Second Division.

The Manchester United match day programme, the *United Review* was first sold at Old Trafford on 31 August 1946.

Programmes had obviously been produced for many years prior to this, but this opening fixture of season 1946-47 was the first time it carried the legend *United Review*, with its famous player and supporter shaking hands logo.

For many years, the programme was only sold inside the ground, as included within its pages was a 'programme token', which first appeared in 1956-57. These were often required to be stuck on token sheets and presented at the ticket office as proof that you had been to a game. This was in order to purchase a ticket for a forthcoming cuptie, big league fixture or indeed a Cup Final.

Programmes were popular with the match going public and for the World Club Championship match against Estudiantes on 16 October 1968, a record 74,680 copies were sold. Almost one for every person who attends a capacity crowd fixture at Old Trafford today.

CHARITY SHIELD
RECORD MAKERS

Manchester United played in the very first F. A. Charity Shield (now the Community Shield) fixture in 1908, when, as League Champions, they played Southern League Champions Queens Park Rangers at Stamford Bridge.

The first game was played on 27 April 1908, when the two sides drew 1-1, but in a replay, on 29 August United ran out 4-0 winners. This is the only time that the fixture has gone to a replay.

Since then, United can claim the record number of wins with 19: 15 outright and 4 shared (at the time of writing).

They can also claim to have the player who has scored the most goals in one Charity Shield fixture, with Harold Halse notching six goals in the 8-4 victory over Southern League side Swindon Town on 25 September 1911.

United were also involved in the only Charity Shield fixture which saw a goalkeeper scoring within normal play. Tottenham Hotspur's Pat Jennings clearing the ball from his goal at Old Trafford's Stretford End and watching it bounce over the head of United's Alex Stepney at the opposite end of the pitch during the 3-3 draw in August 1967.

EVERTON
EVERTON
EVERTON

FACT **76**

Of all the teams that Manchester United have faced over the years, there is one that they have played in more competitions than any other and that is Everton.

They have faced the Goodison Park side in eight different first team competitive competitions – the First Division, Premier League, FA Cup, Football League Cup, FA Charity Shield, Inter Cities Fairs Cup, the Screen Sport Super Cup and the Mercantile Credit Centenary Trophy.

If you really wanted to take it one step further, you could also throw in the First World War tournaments - Lancashire Section War League Principle Tournament and Subsidiary Tournament Southern Section and the Second World War competitions – War Regional League Western Division, North Regional League, League War Cup, Football League Northern Section First Championship, Football League North Second Championship, War League Cup Qualifying Competition and the Football League North.

The likes of the Lancashire Senior Cup could add a further competition, but this tournament would quite often see reserve teams fielded.

77
FIRST LEAGUE CUP
CAMPAIGNS BEST FORGOTTEN

Manchester United's early ventures into the Football League Cup proved rather disastrous.

Entering the competition for the first time in season 1960-61, they were drawn away to Exeter City, with the Fourth Division side holding them to a 1-1. In the replay United were more convincing, winning 4-1. In the second round they were drawn away to Bradford City, then a Third Division club, and once again they struggled against their lesser opponents, losing 2-1.

They did not re-appear in the League Cup until season 1966-67, as it was not compulsory to enter, and drawn away against fellow First Division side Blackpool, they were trounced 5-1.

Semi-finalists in 1969-70 (losing 4-3 on aggregate to Manchester City), and again the following season when they lost 3-2 to Aston Villa, and yet again in 1974-75, losing 3-2 to Norwich City (Villa being a Third Division club and Norwich, like United at the time, in the Second Division).

It was not until 1982-83 that they first reached the Final, losing 2-1 after extra time. They reached the Final again in 1991, losing to Sheffield Wednesday (then in the Second Division) before lifting the trophy for the first time the following year, beating Nottingham Forest 1-0.

Since then they have won the League Cup in one of its various guises a further three times, in 2005-06, 2008-09 and 2009-10.

Modern day football sees most clubs having at least three different strips. One for home games, another for away and a third a mere money making venture to wear on an odd occasion. Over the years, United have worn a vast array of shirts, with a breakdown as follows.

Under the Newton Heath banner, they are recorded as wearing red and white quarters, while the *Athletic News* mentions that the club colours were green and gold, with early photographs showing the players in striped or a green shirt with gold trimmings. It is also debated that the 'quartered' shirts were also green and gold.

In 1896 it was a plain white shirt and dark blue shorts, but when the club became Manchester United in 1902 they chose to play in red shirts, white shorts and black socks. Change shirts of white and blue stripes were also adopted.

In 1922 a white shirt with a red 'v' became the new club kit for a five year period, before once again reverting back to the plain red, with white for a change if required.

In 1932, in the hope that a change of playing attire would bring a change of luck, maroon and white hooped shirts were worn, but after the Second World War, it was back to the good old red and white, which remain to this day, although the change strips that have been worn would probably take up a book on their own!

Although United have had a wide array of different styles of playing kit over the years, they, unlike many clubs in the modern game have not gone through a large number of actual shirt sponsors. Such deals can bring in millions of pounds, due to the obvious fact that having your company name on the Manchester United shirt guarantees you instant exposure to millions across the world.

But since shirt sponsorship became the norm in the late seventies, there have to date only been five names on those red, or whatever colour of shirt, United happen to be playing in on a particular day. These have been *Sharp Electronics*, *Vodaphone*, *AIG*, *AON* and the current *Chevrolet*. The *AON* agreement was a four year deal for £80m but the deal with *Chevrolet* was at the time a world-record. Signed in 2012 on terms of £47m per year!

A GREY DAY
GIVES UNITED
THE BLUES

Having just mentioned United's playing kit in its different variations over the years, it is worth noting one particular shirt that had a rather brief lifespan, the infamous grey one of the 1995-96 season .

It proved to be something of an unlucky choice of colour as they failed to win a game whilst wearing it. Four of that seasons six defeats, against Aston Villa, Arsenal, Liverpool and Southampton all occurred when wearing the grey shirt. At Nottingham Forest they did manage to secure a point in a 1-1 draw. A friendly was won in Malaysia playing in grey, but this was the only success.

But it was against Southampton, that the grey shirt finally met its end. With United losing 3-0 at half time, they were given special permission by the referee to change their shirts and play the second forty-five minutes in blue and white. It made little difference as the game finished 3-1.

This was the second time in the club's history that they had made a half time change of kit, with the previous one coming way back in February 1903 in an FA Cup tie against Everton when they changed from their normal red to blue and white, but on that occasion it was simply due to the weather conditions.

THE SEASON
EVERYONE WAS
SHORT CHANGED

United's shortest season on record is that of 1939-40.

Having finished the previous season in 14th position in the First Division, the club were looking for an improved position in the following campaign. But, with only three games played, a 4-0 opening day victory against Grimsby Town at Old Trafford, a 1-1 draw against Chelsea at Stamford Bridge and a 2-0 defeat, again in London, this time against Charlton Athletic, the season as such was called to a halt with the advent of the Second World War.

A Regional War League replaced the fixtures and with players being called up for the forces, team often had a number of guest players included in their line ups.

If war had not been declared, who knows what would have come United's way, as that Western Division of the War League saw Walter Crickmer's United in devastating form, in what is arguably there highest scoring season in history.

They scored six goals in three consecutive fixtures, against Tranmere Rovers, Stockport County and New Brighton, while earlier in the season, they scored 24 in four games. Eight against Port Vale, four against Tranmere Rovers, Seven against Stockport County and five against Wrexham. Strangely, they were only to finish in fourth place.

TV AND THE
BIG SCREEN

The first time United featured in a live televised game was back in 1948 and the FA Cup Final against Blackpool at Wembley, shown by the BBC. But due to television being something of a novelty in those somewhat distant days, it was only shown in the London area. The BBC also showed the second half of the 1952 FA Charity Shield match against Newcastle United live from Old Trafford.

United's first appearance on the BBC *Sports Special* programme, and indeed the first game at Old Trafford to be televised, was on 7 April 1956 - their championship decider against Blackpool

It was ITV, who managed to obtain the rights to cover a United game at Old Trafford, with the European Cup semi-final tie against Real Madrid. Finding suitable camera positions were the big problem as there was no camera position inside the ground like today. In the end, they positioned them at the back of the terracing behind the goals and along the side of the pitch. This was the first United game to be shown live on television.

There is, however, footage in existence of the 1911 FA Cup Final replay between Bradford City and Newcastle United which was played at the ground.

United's first appearances on *Match of the Day* was on 5 September 1964 away at Fulham, a 2-1 defeat.

For those without television, they could of course visit their local cinema, as the popular *Pathe News* showed snippets of numerous United games over the years, along with shots of the players training, as well as the Munich disaster.

No *Pathe News* today, but you can get all the United action you want on the club's own television channel MUTV.

TIME NOT
ON OUR SIDE

Games are played over the course of ninety minutes, with additional time for stoppages, or 'Fergie time' as it was referred to if Manchester United were playing during Ferguson's reign. With cup-ties an additional thirty minutes, along with penalty kicks might stretch the game out even more, but what about playing over the course of two days?

A little misleading perhaps, as no United fixture has ever lasted anywhere near 48 hours, not even Sir Alex Ferguson could have got that amount of time added on to ensure his team won!

But on two occasions United games have begun one day and been concluded the following one. During the American tour of 1950, United faced Swedish side Jonköpping at the Polo Grounds in New York on 9 June. Kicking off at 10.15pm, it did not end until 12.05am the following morning. But perhaps the most common instance of a 'two day' fixture was in May 2008 and the Champions League final against Chelsea in Moscow.

Kicking off at 8.45pm in the UK, this was 22.45pm in Moscow and with the ninety minutes, the extra time and then penalties followed by the cup presentation. It was well into the following morning before the game finally came to an end.

FACT 83 "GET YOUR PROGRAMMES HERE. ONLY £20,000!"

Manchester United is arguably the most popular club in the world and a considerable number of its supporters collect memorabilia and programmes relating to the club.

It is the latter that many find more appealing, but if this is something you are considering becoming involved in, think again, as some of those programmes from a bygone age are difficult to come by, while others are rather expensive.

Paying record transfer fees for players is something the club is well accustomed to, but even United programmes set world records. The 1909 FA Cup Final against Bristol City sold in May 2012 for £23,500. The previous record being £21,850 for the 1889 Cup Final.

Two of the most sought after United programmes comes from within a few days of each other from February 1958. The one every collector wants is that for the match in Belgrade, against Red Star, the last match played by the immortal 'Busby Babes' before the Munich disaster. The other is a United home programme dated 8 February and number 20 for that season, covering the first Division fixture against Wolverhampton Wanderers.

Due to the crash, this match was postponed, but the printing of the programmes had already begun when news of the crash began to filter through.

Printing was stopped and most of the copies destroyed, although some did survive and are eagerly sought after today.

84

UNITED'S SENIOR CUP MOMENTS

Today Manchester United contest the likes of the Premier League, the FA Cup, more often than not the Champions League and to a lesser degree the Football League Cup.

Back in the club's early days the quest for honours was not something that was expected by the support as they looked on enviously at other clubs, with the competitions on offer certainly not as grand as those of today.

But even for the fledgling Newton Heath club there were trophies to compete for. In 1886 the local engraver was called upon to etch the name of Newton Heath for the first time following the club's success in the Manchester Cup. This was the first trophy won by the club.

This competition became the Manchester Senior Cup in 1888 and the initial competition was won by the Heathens, who went on to win it three seasons in succession.

Between the mid-sixties and the 1990's, the interest in the competition disappeared, but it soon became part of the reserve team's fixture list with United enjoying continued success in recent seasons.

REACHING FOR
THE SKY... BLUE

Inter club rivalry is an integral part of football, adding to the electric match day atmosphere. It is a rivalry that could have been created during several memorable tussles, such as the FA Cup semi-finals between Manchester United and Leeds United, along with of course the Yorkshire/Lancashire involvement, which lingers on today despite the two sides no longer playing in the same division.

There is also the United – Liverpool rivalry, a more modern day thing, when Liverpool would rule the roost, but more often than not could not get the better of their Lancashire rivals.

But for United's long term rivals and even more so today, it is Manchester City, the team they want to beat more than any other.

Up to this season (2012-13) there have been 165 league and cup fixtures between the two sides, United winning 69, City 46, with 50 draws.

The first meeting at league level was on 3 November 1894 at Hyde Road, with Newton Heath running out 5-2 winners. They were also to score five in the first FA Cup meeting, on 3 October 1891 at North Road, winning the First Round tie 5-1.

When it comes to the highest victory margin, it is City who come out on top with two 6-1 triumphs, both at Old Trafford, while the best United can manage is 5-0, although during the Second World War, they did record a 7-1 victory, the highest recorded between the two clubs.

THE GAME THE REF NEARLY ENDED

FACT 86

Segregation at games was not always something that occurred, with supporters of different clubs allowed to mix freely on the terraces. Up to the mid-sixties, this was rarely a problem, but soon running battles became something of the norm.

Locally rivalry was always going to create tension, but it was not until season 1973-74 that it was decided to segregate the supporters completely for a City – United game. This was to be nothing more than a roped off area down part of Maine Road's Kippax Street enclosure, with policemen in the no-man's land in between.

Ironically, the match on 1 December did not take place, but in the re-arranged fixture on 13 March, it was not so much the opposition supporters who needed to be kept apart, but the players, as the game was almost abandoned.

Lou Macari and Mike Doyle tussled in midfield and were booked before being ordered off by referee Clive Thomas. Both players refused to go and after much arguing, the referee picked up the ball and walked off, telling both teams to do likewise.

Once in the dressing rooms, Thomas informed both teams that unless Macari and Doyle remained in there, the game would not continue. Fortunately both players stayed put and the game continued, ending in a no score draw.

THE NOT SO
NEUTRAL REF?

It is not unusual for supporters to consider a certain referee is biased towards the opposition, but few, if any of the match officials ever reveal what team they supported in their youth, or indeed still have a soft spot for.

Four match officials who might have had a leaning towards United were Herbert Dale, George Owen, Herbert Bamlett or John Bentley. The first two mentioned were former Newton Heath players who went on to become match officials, while Bentley, who was United secretary between 1912 and 1916, was also a well-respected referee.

Herbert Bamlett on the other hand, became the United manager in 1927, filling the post until 1931. Prior to this, he had refereed at the highest level and was the youngest FA Cup final referee at 32, when he took charge of the 1914 final between Burnley and Liverpool. He was also referee for the 1909 FA Cup quarter-final tie between Burnley and Manchester United at Turf Moor, a match which ended in controversy when he called the proceedings to a halt with 18 minutes remaining due to a snow storm. Burnley at the time were winning 1-0 and ironically lost the re-arranged match 3-2.

GOING FOR
A SONG

There are records and there are records, with Manchester United not simply content to strive to the top of the footballing charts, but also the pop charts.

Songs involving the United playing squad of the time with the titles such as 'Onward Sexton's Soldiers', 'Glory Glory Man United', 'We All Follow Man United' and 'Come On You Reds', the latter with rock band Status Quo, all attempted to hit the number one spot, but only the latter song did and for two whole weeks in 1994.

There have also been records issued about the team and players by individuals, such as Don Fardon's 'Belfast Boy' about George Best in 1970. But perhaps the most famous Manchester United musical record is the 1956 recording of the 'Manchester United Calypso' sung by Edric Connor who intriguingly was the Royal Shakespeare Company's first black actor. This song is still a match day anthem for the United supporters.

MAN UNITED 7
STOKE CITY 7

It is not unusual to face the same opposition in more than the normal two league fixtures during a season, as there are the two domestic cup competitions, or if it was one of the more successful sides, there is always the possibility of facing them in a European tie.

However, the most times Manchester United have played against one club in a particular season is seven, against Stoke City, during season 1971-72.

There were the two First Division fixtures, at Old Trafford on 29 April and at the Victoria Ground on 11 December. The two clubs were also drawn against each other in the 6th round of the FA Cup, playing out a 1-1 draw at Old Trafford, with Stoke winning the replay at the Victoria Ground 2-1 after extra time.

In the football League Cup, they were again drawn against each other, this time in round four. On 27 October, they drew 1-1 at Old Trafford, with the replay at Stoke ending 0-0 after extra time. In the second replay, again at Stoke, United lost 2-1.

If you followed United away from home at that time, you would have had a fifth visit to the Victoria Ground, as United played West Bromwich Albion there on 23 August, as United were forced to play their opening two home fixtures of that season away from Old Trafford due to a knife throwing incident the previous season against Newcastle United.

SOME YOU LOSE, SOME YOU DRAW

FACT **90**

Manchester United's worst run of games without a victory in the Football League is 16, on two occasions, between 3 November 1928 and 9 February 1929 and between 19 April and 25 October 1930.

During the 1928-29 sequence, there were four draws and five odd-goal defeats, with 6-1 the biggest reversal. In the latter poor run, there were only two draws, while they conceded five and six on two occasions each and seven on another. The 6-2 defeat at Chelsea on September 6th, the 6-0 home defeat by Huddersfield Town four days later and the 7-4 defeat, again at home, this time against Newcastle United, are the worst sequence of results in the clubs history.

The 1930 sequence, which obviously spanned two seasons brought only one victory, while the unproductive run during the 1928-29 season was actually interrupted by a 3-0 home win over Port Vale in the FA Cup on 12 January.

That same period also produced United's longest spell without a home League victory – 9 games, but again this was interrupted by that 'shock' FA Cup victory against Port Vale.

Between 26 April 1930, a 3-1 defeat at Leeds United and 21 February 1931, a 4-1 defeat at Arsenal, United lost seventeen away fixtures in a row. A further four games were played before they managed to obtain that illusive victory. They did, however, like in the previously mentioned seasons, manage a win in the FA Cup, defeating Stoke City on 19 January 1931 in a Third Round second replay.

MUFC = PFA

The modern day Professional Footballers Association have Manchester United players to be grateful for, for their initial involvement in setting up the organisation in the December 1907 with footballers of that period demanding greater rights.

An increase in their £4 per week maximum wage being a major factor. Much to the Football Association's annoyance, the likes of Charlie Roberts, Billy Meredith and Herbert Broomfield were at the forefront of organising a meeting in the Imperial Hotel Manchester, with some 500 fellow professionals turning up. Bloomfield was named as secretary on a wage of £150 per year.

The Football Associations were quick in an effort to nip the organisation in the bud before it could establish itself, having a clause written into player's contracts, saying that they would not join the 'Union'.

The United contingent stood firm and were eventually banned from using the club facilities and posed for newspaper photographers in a team group under the banner 'The Outcasts'.

On the eve of the 1909-10 season, the Football Association backed down, preventing chaos, giving the players a famous victory.

Over the years, a number of United, or former United players have held the position of Chairman of the Professional Footballers Association – Charlie Roberts (1919-21), Noel Cantwell (1966-67), Alan Gowling (1980-82), Steve Coppell (1982-84) and Garth Crooks (1988-90).

SIGNED IN EXCHANGE FOR ICE-CREAM!

Multi-million pound transfers are commonplace today but Manchester United were involved in two of the strangest transfers on record.

On 7 February 1925 Clapton Orient travelled north from London to Manchester for a Second Division fixture, but prior to the match, the united officials made enquires to the Orient counterparts as to the availability of their inside forward Albert Pape.

A fee was quickly agreed and a telephone call made to the Football League, who approved the deal. So instead of changing in the 'away' dressing room, Pape was

introduced to his new team mates in the 'home' one and ran onto the pitch as a United player while also scoring in his new teams 4-2 victory.

Two years later, in May 1927, United signed Hughie McLenahan from Stockport County. Nothing unusual in that, but the transfer fee was three freezers of ice cream!

United were keen on McLenahan before the player had signed for Stockport, but with a hint that he might be available. County were planning a fund raising bazaar, United jack-of-all-trades Louis Rocca, whose family had a well-known ice cream business in Manchester, donated the freezers of ice cream to Stockport and in exchange Hugh McLenahan was released from his amateur contract and made his way to Old Trafford.

93

THEY DAY UNITED SURVIVED THE DROP TO THE THIRD DIVISION

Manchester United in the Third Division is quite unthinkable. Indeed, there will be many of the present day supporters completely unaware that the club has endured some dismal days in the Second Division, even as recently as the mid-seventies.

But back in 1920s and 1930s, United led something of a yo-yo existence, moving between Divisions One and Two with some regularity. But in season 1933-34 it began to look as though Manchester United would be playing third Division football for the first time the following season.

One win in the five April fixtures left the club on the brink of relegation, with only a victory over fellow relegation strugglers Millwall on the final Saturday of the season being the only thing that could save them from the drop.

On the morning of that final Saturday, United were second bottom, Lincoln City already relegated, with Millwall and Swansea only a point in front.

In a season that had seen 38 players used, it was down to just 11 to prevent the drop, a total reduced to 10 early in the game at the Den, when Hine was injured and simply limped up and down the wing.

Despite this handicap, Manley scored before half time, while Cape added a second after the interval. The Londoners could do little to turn the match around. United were safe.

THE FIRST
PENALTY SHOOT-OUT

No one likes to endure penalty shoot-outs, least of all John Terry, but they have become part and parcel of the modern game.

With Manchester United at the forefront of most things – first English team to win the European Cup, first to win the treble, first British side to be crowned World Champions, it is not surprising that they were involved in the first penalty shoot-out in English football.

Participating in the 1970-71 Watney Cup pre-season tournament, (a short lived competition which saw the top two teams from each division who had scored the most goals, but were not involved in European football or had won promotion), United were paired with Reading in the first round, winning 3-2.

In round two, they faced Hull City and at the end of ninety minutes the score stood at 1-1 with Law scoring for United. In order to determine who went through to the final, it was down to penalty kicks.

Best, Kidd, Charlton and Morgan all scored for United to enable them to go through to the final 5-4. They were, however, unable to celebrate winning the trophy, as they lost 4-1 at Derby County in the final.

United also became the first top flight club to be knocked out of the FA Cup on penalty kicks. Having drawn 0-0 at Southampton in the FA Cup fourth round in January 1992, the two sides met at Old Trafford in the replay, where the score was 2-2 after ninety minutes and an thirty minutes extra time. It was down to penalty kicks in front of the Stretford End, with the visitors winning 4-2.

THE SPOT ON
PENALTY TAKERS

When it comes to taking penalties many would not wish to encounter a 'John Terry' moment and they would make sure they were well down the queue come penalty shootout time. In recent seasons, there have been a number of misses from the spot, while over the years, others have shown little fear in stepping forward, putting the ball on the spot and placing it past goalkeepers with much regularity.

Eric Cantona scored 18 penalties, including two in the 1994 FA Cup final against Chelsea, while missing only 2 during his five year United career. With all but two of those spot kicks, the goalkeeper dived the wrong way.

Other notable spot kick experts were Albert Quixall, who also scored 18, although missing 4, Steve Bruce with 17 successes and 5 misses, while Charlie Mitten, who scored a hat trick of penalties against Aston Villa on 8 March 1950, scored 16, with 4 misses.

Gerry Daly scored 4 penalties in three games in the opening fixtures of the 1974-75 season, the Irishman scoring 17 penalties in all, while missing only once. Arguably the best post-war average.

WITH YOUTH
ON THEIR SIDE

Manchester United won the inaugural FA Youth Cup competition in season 1952-53, defeating Wolverhampton Wanderers 9-3 on aggregate (7-1 at Old Trafford and drawing 2-2 away) and went on to win the competition over the course of the next four seasons.

They met Wolves again in 1953-54 Final winning 5-4 on aggregate (4-4 at home and winning 1-0 away); West Bromwich Albion 7-1 on aggregate in the 1954-55 competition (4-0 at home and 3-0 away); Chesterfield 4-3 over the two-legged Final of 1955-56 (3-2 at home and 1-1 away), and West Ham United 8-2 over the two games in season 1956-57 (3-2 away and 5-0 at home).

With players such as Duncan Edwards, Eddie Colman, David Pegg, Liam Whelan and Bobby Charlton in those early line ups, it was perhaps not surprising that there was a considerable gulf between United and their opponents. This was obvious, not just in those Finals, but in the early round of the competition itself, with Bexleyheath and Welling being trounced 11-1 in March 1956 and Plymouth Argyle 9-0 a year earlier. Nantwich were beaten by an incredible 23-0 in November 1952 -a record score line in the competition which will stand for all time.

Strangely, it was not until season 1963-64 that they would win the trophy again, defeating Swindon Town 5-2 over the two legs, with a team that included a certain George Best.

There is always time added on for injuries, substitutions or whatever, but the duration of a football match is set at ninety minutes, unless it is a cup tie that goes into extra time, or if there is a major incident and the police or officials feel that it is unsafe to continue.

Manchester United have been involved in a couple of such First Division fixtures that did not last the expected duration. One in 1962, the other in 1974.

The latter is ingrained in United's history. On 27 April 1974, with United staring relegation to the Second Division in the face, they were due to play neighbours Manchester City in the penultimate fixture of the season. Needing a victory to have any hope of survival, the Old Trafford crowd were stunned when former idol of the Stretford End Denis Law, now a City player, scored with an innocuous back heel, eight minutes from time.

A mass pitch invasion followed, more in the hope of having the game abandoned and replayed than anything else and when a second invasion followed soon afterwards, the referee called a halt to the game.

It was never replayed and with other results not going United's way, they were relegated.

The first fixture not to be completed, also played at Old Trafford, was on 22 December 1962, when the first Division fixture against Arsenal was abandoned because of fog after fifty-seven minutes. This game was of course replayed at a later date.

THE PLAYER-MANAGER

United have only ever had one player-manager as such and he was Clarence 'Lal' Hilditch, who occupied the mangers office during season 1926-27, taking over from the suspended John Chapman.

Hilditch had joined the club from Altrincham in January 1916, playing regularly in the regional leagues during the First World War, going on to win Football League and FA honours. His only England appearance was in a 'Victory' international. Although his playing career with United was to stretch to over 300 appearances, he was never to win any domestic honours during his thirteen seasons with the club.

Upon taking over the position of manager, he was somewhat reluctant to select himself, playing in only seventeen of the thirty odd games in charge.

Although Hilditch was the only 'official' player manager, Wilf McGuinness, who managed the club between 1955-56 and 1959-60 made 85 appearances, while both Tommy Docherty and Sir Alex Ferguson took to the field during first team friendly fixtures on club tours. Sir Matt Busby did likewise in a junior friendly at the Cliff.

And let's not forget that Ryan Giggs became interim player-manager when Moyes was sacked in April 2014.

IF UNITED HAD £150
THE BUSBY ERA MAY
NEVER HAVE HAPPENED

FACT **99**

Matt Busby may well have become a Manchester United player a number of years before he joined the club as manager.

Belshill born Busby, played all his professional football south of the border, joining Manchester City in February 1928, moving to Liverpool for £8,000 in 1936.

While he was at Maine Road and not exactly setting the world on fire with his performances, across the city, United were going through something of an injury crisis and such was the shortage of players that Louis Rocca approached Manchester City manager Peter Hodge and asked if he could "borrow one player for Saturday". When asked who it was, the United man replied "Matt Busby".

With little hesitation, Hodge replied, "give me £150 and you can have him". "We don't have 150 cents never mind £150" replied the down hearted Rocca and so the player remained at City.

Had he moved there was the distinct possibility that Busby might never have become manager of Manchester United later in his career.

100 A HANDFUL OF MANAGERS AND A HATFUL OF SUCCESS

Some football clubs have had more managers in one season, than Manchester United have had in its entire history.

In the early days of the Newton Heath club, the man in charge went under the title of club secretary, with A. H. Albut the first between 1890 and 1900. He was succeeded by James West, 1900 -1903, with Ernest Mangnall taking over the office until 1912, guiding his team to that first trophy success, the First Division championship in 1908.

Secretary J.J. Bentley took the helm for a couple of years before Jack Robson became the man who is regarded as the club's first actual manager who took over in 1914.

Robson resigned in 1921, with John Chapman moving in to enjoy a five year reign before he was suspended by the Football Association from having any involvement in football due to alleged improper conduct. Full details of what Chapman was meant to have done remain a mystery to this day.

Clarence Hilditch enjoyed a brief spell as player-manager between October 1926 and April 1927, before Herbert Bamlett was appointed. The former referee remained in charge until 1931, when the club secretary Walter Crickmer held the fort until A. Scott Duncan moved south from Cowdenbeath in 1932.

Duncan resigned 14 games into season 1938-39 to join Ipswich Town and again Walter Crickmer stepped into the void, guiding the team through the Second World War years before the arrival of a certain Matt Busby in February 1946.

Busby, along with Jimmy Murphy who enjoyed a brief spell in charge following the Munich disaster, laid the foundations of the Manchester United of today and remained in charge until stepping down in 1969. He was, however, to step back into the Old Trafford hot-seat during 1970-71, as his replacement, Wilf McGuinness failed to live up to expectation.

In June 1971, Frank O'Farrell took over as manager, lasting until December 1972, before Tommy Docherty swept into office. Flamboyant, but not exactly blessed with success, the controversial Scot was sacked in 1977 and was replaced by Dave Sexton.

Sexton, although taking the club close to the coveted league championship was in turn sacked in April 1981, despite having won his last seven games. His style of football blamed for his eventual downfall.

Larger than life Ron Atkinson was the club's next manager and although not the first choice of the United directors, he did win the FA Cup on two occasions, but like his predecessors, he could not claim that elusive First Division crown.

Sacked following a 4-1 League Cup defeat at Southampton, he was replaced by Alex Ferguson in November 1986 and despite a rocky start to life after Aberdeen, the board of directors thankfully continued to back the Glaswegian, who went on to take Manchester United through its most successful years.

It has been a somewhat bumpy road for United since Ferguson's retirement in 2013, with his short-lived replacement David Moyes inevitably having so much to live up to that life was always going to be tough. Despite Ryan Giggs acting as interim for a month, Dutchman Louis van Gaal was appointed in July 2014. The first United manager not to have descended from the British Isles.

The 100 Facts Series

Celtic, *Steve Horton*   978-1-908724-10-6
Chelsea, *Kristian Downer*   978-1-908724-11-3
Liverpool, *Steve Horton*   978-1-908724-13-7
Manchester City, *Steve Horton*   978-1-908724-14-4
Manchester United, *Iain McCartney*   978-1-908724-15-1
Newcastle United, *Steve Horton*   978-1-908724-16-8

ABOUT CHILDLINE

You can contact *ChildLine* about anything - no problem is too big or too small. If you're feeling worried, scared, stressed or just want to talk to someone you can contact *ChildLine*. We're here to offer information and support whenever you need us.

We understand that it can be difficult to trust someone and tell them about what is happening or how you are feeling.

We want to help you feel confident when you use *ChildLine* and show what you can expect from us.

How can I contact *ChildLine*?

Call free on 0800 1111 or visit http://www.childline.org.uk/

---

www.childlinerocks.co.uk

ChildLine Rocks is an annual charity rock concert organised under the auspices of *ChildLine 20*, an independent committee set up to raise £2,000,000 for *ChildLine* to celebrate 20 years of *ChildLine's* existence.

Lightning Source UK Ltd.
Milton Keynes UK
UKOW06f1306190315

248143UK00001B/10/P